GOLDEN PROPORTION

WITH FIBONACCI SERIES AND WHERE TO FIND THEM

DIAGRAMS

SPIRAL AND
ISLAMIC
LABYRINTHS,
MANDALAS

BY MILENA

M PUBLISHING

CONTENTS

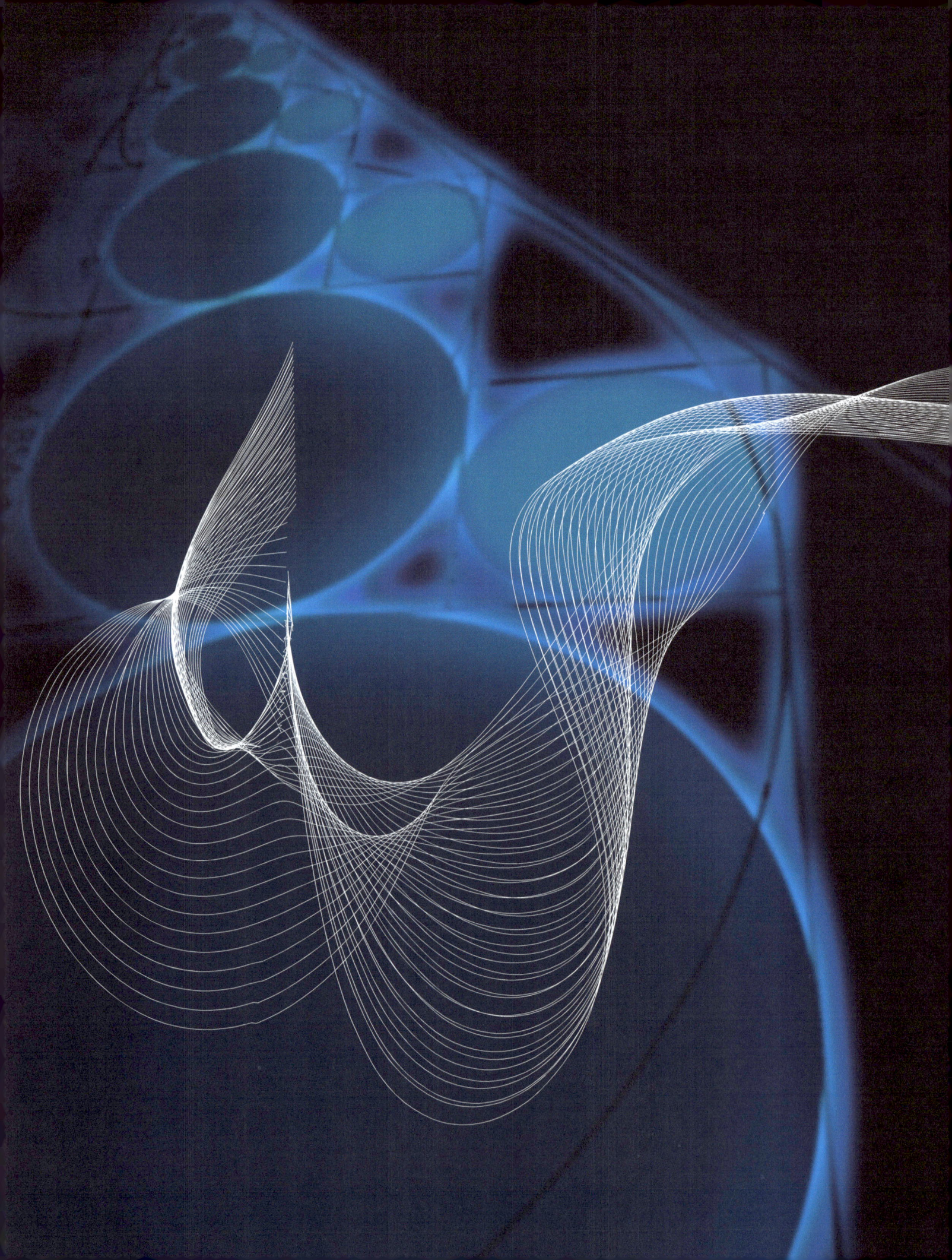

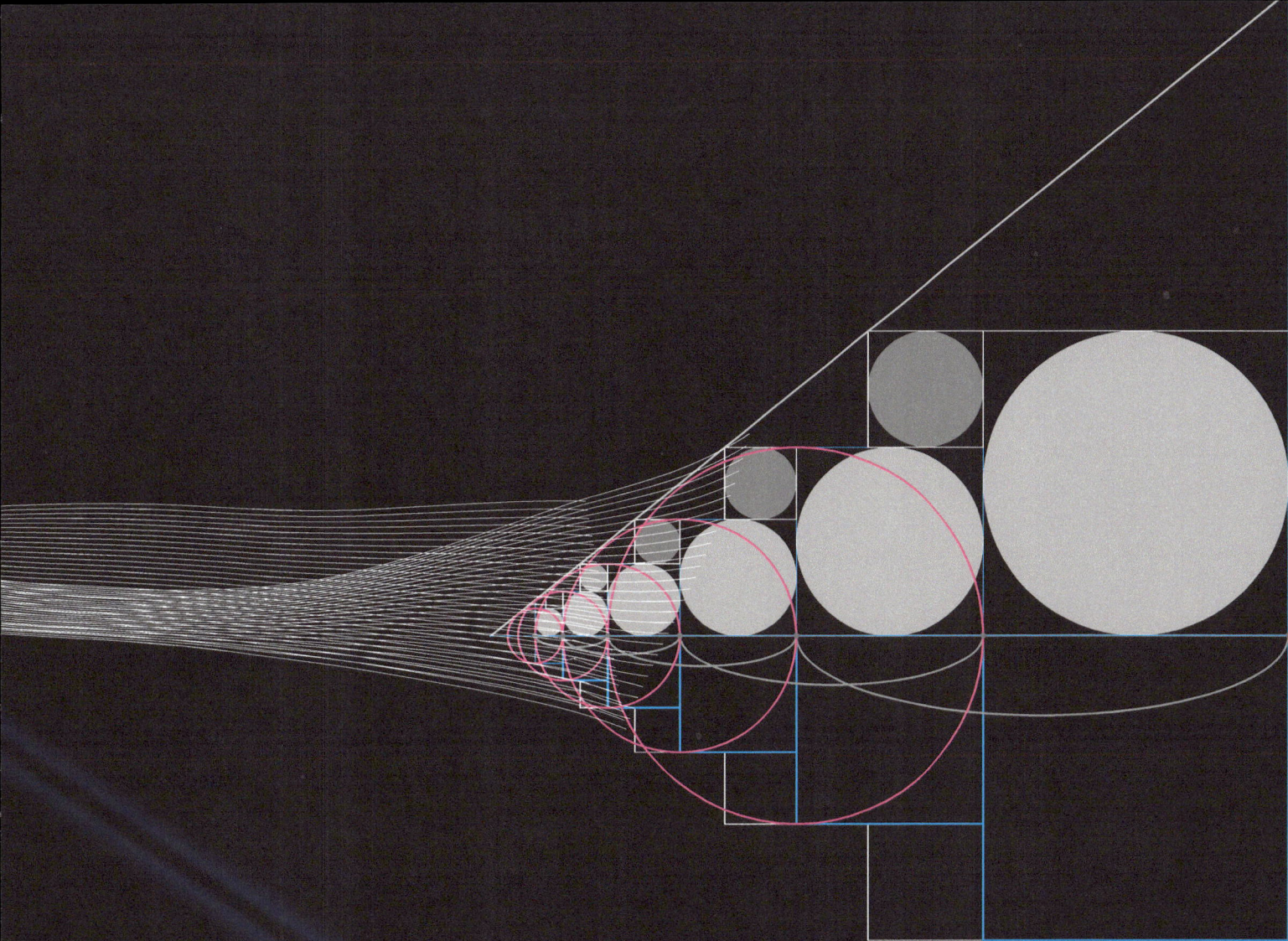

GOLDEN PROPORTION

The best bond is the one that affects the closest unity between itself and the terms it is combining; and this is best done by a continued geometrical proportion.

Plato[1-1]

DIVISION WITH THE REFERENCE

A proportion is a relationship of equality between two ratios whereby the ratio is a comparison of two values. A proportion is expressed as: *a:b=c:d* or numerically, for example, 3:9=11:33.

The ratio between a short wave and a long wave in which it can best be embedded, is Φ or the golden proportion. This is the best nesting algorithm for waves to share spin non-destructively.

Daniel Winter[1-2]

The given example features a proportion made of four different terms which the Pythagoreans called a *discontinuous proportion*. If we reduce our consideration to three different terms, we get what the Greeks considered to be a *continuous proportion*.

A continuous proportion, where extremes are related through and reconciled by a common element *(b)*, stands as: *a:b=b:c*. If *(b)* is the perceiver or thinker, this proportion represents an awareness in which the perceiver or thinker experiences himself/herself in relation to the external elements *(a)* and *(c)*. At this stage there is no awareness of unity or of belonging to the whole.

A specific form of the continuous proportion that comes with further abstraction of thinking, and a consequent reduction of different terms, is a proportion with two different terms. The only case where such a proportion is possible is: *a:b=b:(a+b)* – *where the smaller term is to the larger term the same as the larger term is to the sum of the small and large terms (unity).* Or, in geometrical terms – *there is only one way to divide a line (c) into two unequal parts which are in proportion to the whole and that is when the smaller part (a) to the larger part (b) is the same as the larger part is to their sum (c)* (Fig. 1.1).

This particular proportion is called the *golden proportion*. It is a mathematical formula of an organic unity. The *golden proportion* informs us that the relationship between terms *(a)* and *(b)* is only truly harmonious if it is equal to the relationship between the larger term *(b)* and their joint value, effort or sum *(a+b)*. Such a strong bond, togetherness, or oneness, is achieved only through the ratio known as the *golden number* or *Φ*.

As shown in figure 1.1, the *golden proportion (c)* is 1.618 times *(b)* (c=1.618b) while *(b)* is 1.618 times *(a)* (b=1.618a). At the same time *(a)* is 0.618 of *(b)* (a=0.618b) and *(b)* is 0.618 of *(c)* (b=0.618c). The smaller part is also called the *minor (a)* and the bigger one is called the *major (b)*.

When we bisect a line, we can expect to create a *Dyad*. However, that is just an illusion, because it is only the One experiencing itself through the relations of self-aspects. Thus the division into two parts, taking into account the whole which is divided, actually creates a *Triad*. In a division into two uneven terms *(a and b)* through the *golden proportion,* the whole *(c)* directly affiliates itself with the major *(b)* through Φ, while the major *(b)* holds the same ratio with regard to the minor *(a)*. There is only one set of terms (a) and (b), for every given whole (c), when *golden proportion* is possible.

b:a = (a+b):b = Φ = 1.618
a:b = b:(a+b) = 0.618

GOLDEN PROPORTION

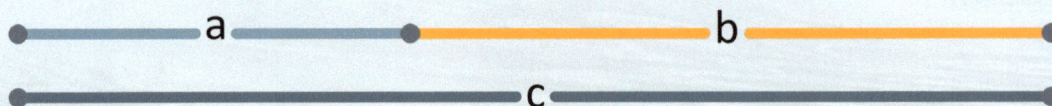

▲ *1.1 – Geometrical division by Φ*

▼ 1.2 – The golden
proportion creates a
potentially infinite
harmonic dynamism of
forms and states

Division
once made into
the *golden propor-
tion* could be contin-
ued *ad infinitum* in two
directions: outwards –
as an expansion through
an increasing geometrical
progression with the de-
nominator Φ (Phi=1.618...)
and inwards – decreas-
ing through a geometri-
cal progression regulated
by φ (phi=0.618...). Both
movements consistently
maintain the properties of
the *golden proportion* and
their order is regulated
by the following rule: in
a *golden proportion,* the
ratio of the minor to the
major is the same as the
ratio of the major to the
sum of the terms, minor
and major.

The quantitative val-
ues of the terms are
not fixed but their
relationship (Φ or
φ) is.

The *golden
proportion* is
the best ex-
ample of co-
herent har-
mony that
proportional
division can
provide.

HISTORY OF Φ

The numerical value of the *golden number* Φ is 1.6180339887499... *ad infinitum*. It is a constant of the godly design that was known to ancient civilisations, such as the Egyptians and Greeks.
Φ is a mathematical description of a perfect balance and beauty. **Plato** (427BC–348BC) considered it to be a key to the physics of the Cosmos and the most significant mathematical relationship.

Over time, this proportion has acquired many names. **Euclid** (365BC–300BC), the great Greek mathematician, in his work *Elements*, referred to it as *the process of dividing a line in the extreme and mean ratio* hence one of its names is the *golden mean*. The word *golden* was used by **Leonardo da Vinci** (1452–1519) who called it *sectio aurea* which means *golden section* in Latin, while **Adolf Zeising** (1810-76) called it the *golden cut*.

Johannes Kepler (1571-1630) used the expression *divine section* and thought it was one of the two greatest treasures in mathematics, resembling a *precious jewel*. According to him, the second treasure was the *theorem of Pythagoras* the value of which he compared with gold.

The glyph Φ was not used until the 1900's when the American mathematician **Mark Barr** named the numerical expression of the *golden proportion* Phi, after the 21st letter (Φ – Phi) of the Greek alphabet. Interestingly, the number 21 is one of the numbers in the *Fibonacci series,* and the letter Φ is the first letter of the name of the great Greek sculptor **Phidias** (c.500BC–c.432BC) famous for the application of the *golden proportion* in his artwork, from the Parthenon to the statue of *Zeus*.

All the names of this unique proportion contain attributes aimed at indicating its ability to establish the order and harmony of the Divine in our world, on its physical, emotional and aesthetical planes. Φ is magical in its insatiable tendency to answer the call of infinity by hurrying towards it. The presence of the *golden proportion* secures beauty, of both function and form, and holds the key to everlasting harmonious unity. Great thinkers of all times, who studied nature and geometry, sensed and understood these properties of the *golden proportion* and celebrated it in their art and architecture.

H

▷ 1.3 – Finding the points of the golden proportion (H and G) relevant to any length of the line AB

VALUE OF Φ AND φ

The value of the ratio Φ is an *irrational number* which can be calculated from:

$$\Phi = \sqrt{1 + \sqrt{1 + \sqrt{1 + \sqrt{1}}}}\ ...$$

$$\Phi = 1 + \cfrac{1}{1 + \cfrac{1}{1 + \cfrac{1}{1 + \cfrac{1}{1 + ...}}}}$$

▲ 1.4 – Two arithmetical representations of Φ. Both reveal an echo of self-similar fragments in the structure of the golden number.

Luca Pacioli (1445-1517) in his book *The Divine Proportion,* published in 1509 and illustrated by **Leonardo da Vinci**, established five properties that made the *golden proportion* worthy of the attribute divine:

1. Unique – as God
2. Always equal to itself – as God
3. Can not be expressed as a rational number, neither can it be defined by words – as God
4. Being made of three terms represents the unity of three – as the *Holy Trinity*
5. Permits the construction of the dodecahedron – an expression of quintessence

GOLDEN PROPORTION

Φ can be obtained by solving the equation $x^2-x^1-x^0=0$, which is the same as $x^2-x-1=0$.

Φ can also be defined through the use of 5 only:

$5^{0.5}\times0.5+0.5=\Phi$ thus it serves for getting the square root of 5: $\sqrt{5}=2\Phi-1$.

The following are some other specifics of Φ:

* If Φ is squared, the resulting number is exactly 1 greater than Φ:

$$\Phi^2 = \Phi+1 \quad 2.618=1.618+1$$

This also means that Φ subtracted from its square value gives 1:

$$\Phi^2 - \Phi =1 \quad 2.618-1.618=1$$

* 0.618 (φ) is a reciprocal of Φ ($1/\Phi$) and also Φ minus 1 (Φ-1):

$$1/\Phi =1/1.618=0.618= \varphi$$
$$\Phi-1=1.618-1=0.618= \varphi$$

Therefore, if 1 is divided by Φ, the resulting number is exactly 1 less than Φ:

$$1/\Phi = \Phi-1$$
$$1/1.618=1.618-1=0.618= \varphi$$

The very definition of the Golden Mean or Divine Phi Ratio is that there is a pure and marvellous symmetry embedded in the numbers, shared wavelengths that can travel from the atom to the universe without being self-destructed, in a sense that are immortal. Only the 1.618 ratio is fractal enough to ensure survival, as it knows how to be self-similar, embeddable, it knows how to be recursive in the micro and macro. That is, there must be a pattern visibly hidden somewhere in this infinite number.

Jain[I-3]

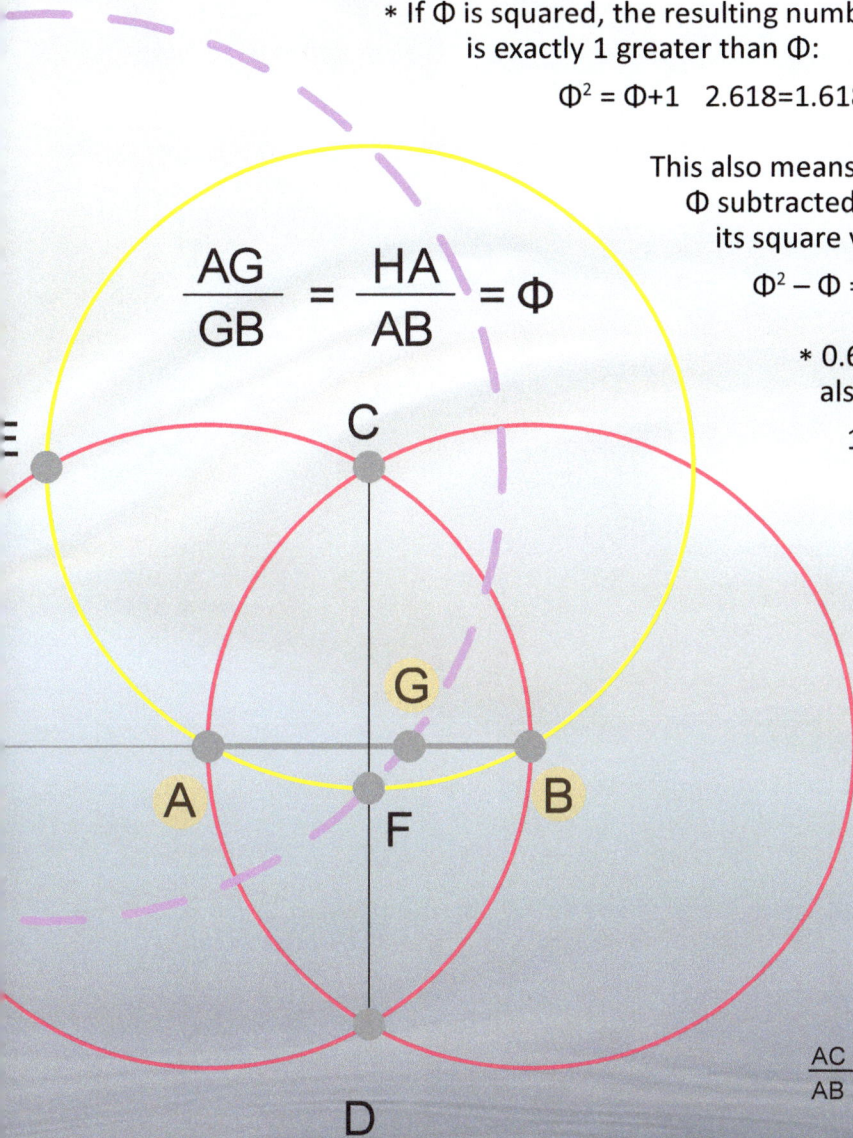

$$\frac{AG}{GB} = \frac{HA}{AB} = \Phi$$

$$\frac{AC}{AB} = \frac{AB}{BC} = \Phi = \frac{1+\sqrt{5}}{2}$$

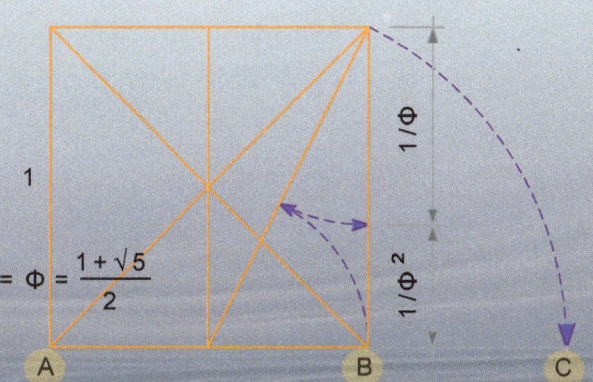

1

$1/\Phi$

$1/\Phi^2$

A B C

▲ *1.5 – Finding the value of Φ, $1/\Phi$ and $1/\Phi^2$*

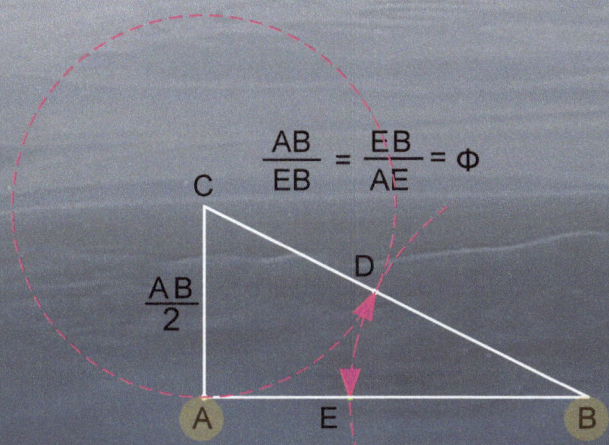

$$\frac{AB}{EB} = \frac{EB}{AE} = \Phi$$

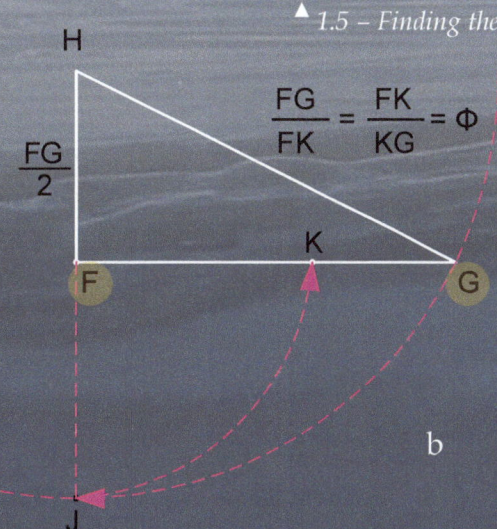

$\frac{AB}{2}$

C D A E B

a

$$\frac{FG}{FK} = \frac{FK}{KG} = \Phi$$

$\frac{FG}{2}$

H F K G J

b

◄ *1.6 (a,b) – Two other ways of dividing into the golden proportion (shown on AB and FG)*

* or:

$\Phi-1/\Phi=1$ 1.618-0.618=1
$1/\Phi+1=\Phi$ 0.618+1=1.618

* also:

$\Phi^x+\Phi^{x+1}=\Phi^{x+2}$, for example:

$\Phi^1+\Phi^{1+1}=\Phi^{1+2}$
$1.618+1.618^2=1.618^3$
$1.618+2.618=4.236=1.618^3$

dividing $\Phi^1+\Phi^{1+1}=\Phi^{1+2}$ by Φ^3 we get:
$1/\Phi^2+1/\Phi=1$ $1-1/\Phi=1/\Phi^2$ 1-0.618=0.382

A numerical series made of numbers in which any number divided by the preceding one is 1.618..., that is Φ, is called a *Φ-series* (0.618, 1.0, 1.618, 2.618, 4.236, 6.854, 11.090, *ad infinitum*). It is the only progression which can be generated either by the addition or through the multiplication of its terms (by Φ).

◈ AND π RELATIONSHIP

Φ belongs to the same family of *irrational numbers* as the numbers π and e. Their relationship is mathematically definable: e times Φ/π equals 1.40000 or Φ=7/5 times π/e, and their arithmetical values can be rounded to: Φ=1.61803, π=3.14159, e=2.71828. These three naturally occurring *irrational numbers* seem to be descending straight from the structure of the Cosmos as representatives of its mysterious power. Getting to know them brings us a better understanding of the creative forces and their constants.

Since both Φ and π evade precise numerical qualification, they are best defined by geometrical methods. One of the ways is shown in figure 1.8. It uses circles as a common ground for both Φ and π. Φ is derived through a construction that involves three concentric circles with a radius of 1, 2 and 4 units. The tangent on the smallest circle is divided by the other circles in the manner of the *golden proportion*. In this geometry π is already present, for it exists in every circle as an invisible link between its radius, circumference and surface area. π is an *irrational number*-factor that guides the behaviour of a curve into achieving a perfect circle.

Interestingly, the secret of two immaculate curves is held by the two *irrational numbers*: π which describes the circle and Φ which does so to the *golden spiral*, a curve which regulates organic growth and numerous other natural processes and phenomena.

Stephen Langton Goulet[1-4], fascinated with the *golden proportion* and π, loves to play with numbers. He noticed an interesting relationship between Φ, π and the *master numbers*.
He performed the following calculations, using some digits of π and Φ, and discovered certain connections with the number 33:

a) 31415 + 1618 = 33033
b) The sum of the first 7 *Fibonacci numbers* equals 33: 1+1+2+3+5+8+13=33.
c) The appearance of zero (0) in π first occurs at the 33rd digit (and again on the 55th and 66th digit).

▲ *1.7 – The Φ-rhythm is mapping the geometry of perfect compression/gravity/memory*

The relationship between π and Φ will be exposed in more detail in chapter *Golden proportion manifested,* under the title *Great Pyramid,* while *golden spiral* will be analysed in the book *Cosmic Diagrams* (chapter *Spirals*).

$$\Phi = \frac{LM}{LA}$$

$$\pi = \frac{C}{2r}$$

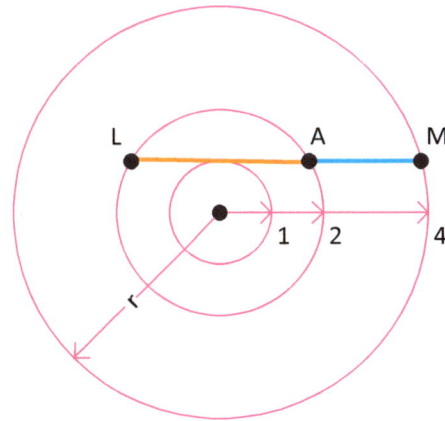

▲ *1.8 – The geometrical determination of Φ and π*

GOLDEN FAMILY

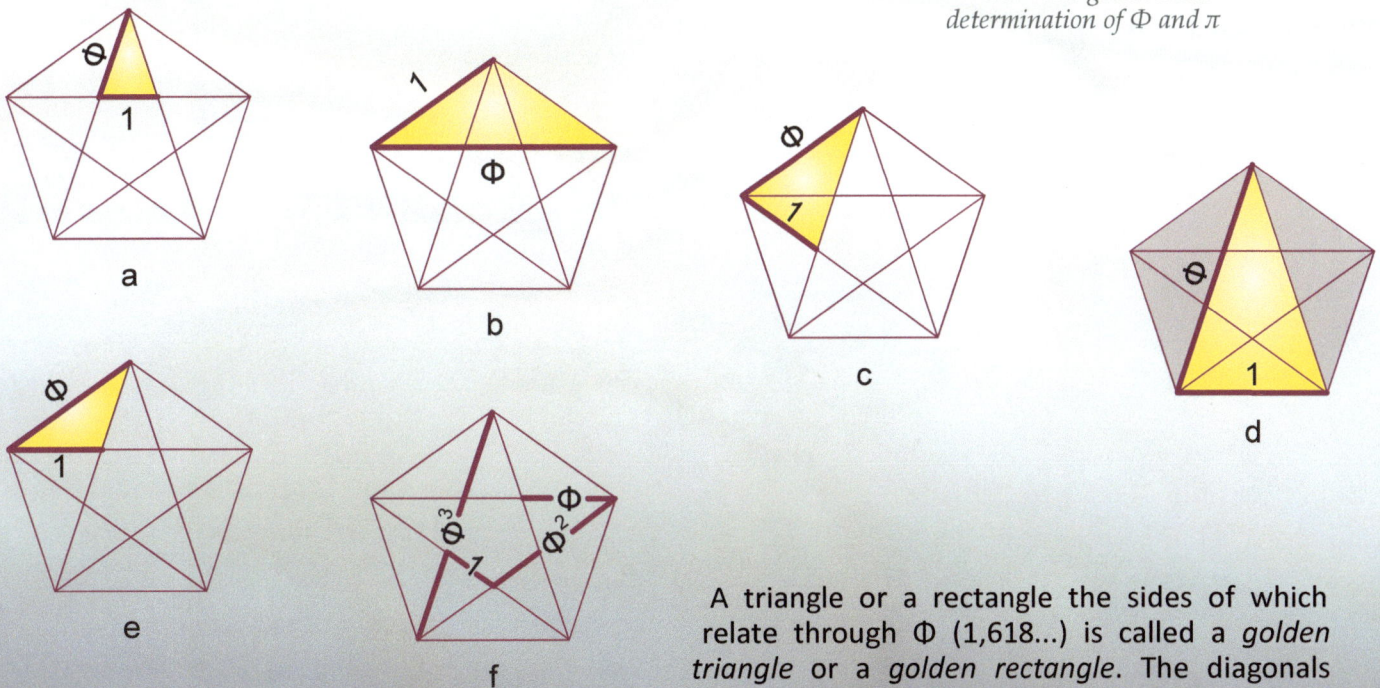

a

b

c

d

e

f

▲ *1.9 – Every triangle of a regular pentagon is a golden triangle*

A triangle or a rectangle the sides of which relate through Φ (1,618...) is called a *golden triangle* or a *golden rectangle*. The diagonals drawn into a regular pentagon form a regular pentagram (five-pointed star), as well as a series of *golden triangles* (Fig. 1.9). Among these triangles is also the best known *golden triangle* – the one with the internal angles of 72°, 72° and 36° (Fig. 1.9a, 1.9c, 1.9d, 1.10, 1.11, 1.15).

The digital root of the interior/exterior angles of a regular pentagon and pentagram is 9:

36: 3+6=9
72: 7+2=9
108: 1+0+8=9

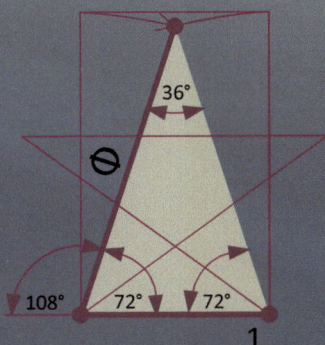

◄ *1.10 – The connection between the golden rectangle and the golden triangle*

► *1.11 – The golden gnomons ADC and ABE*

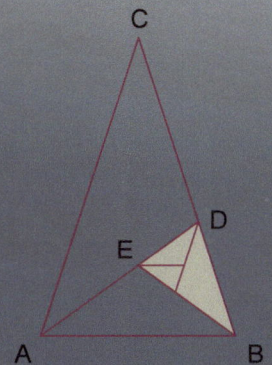

The triangles in figures 1.9b, 1.9e, and the two symmetrically placed ones in figure 1.9d, are called *golden gnomons*. They are also *golden triangles* and in figure 1.11 they appear as triangles ADC and ABE. Further diminution of the triangle EBD will produce an endless number of *golden gnomons*.

The *golden spirals* (left and right turning ones) can be generated from within the *golden triangle* (Fig. 1.14) and the *golden rectangle* (Fig. 1.12).

The *golden bowl* is a form born from a regular pentagon/pentagram. It is a geometry often used in the design of ancient Egyptian and Greek vases and is made of two *golden gnomons* (Fig. 1.12).

There is also an angle called the *golden angle*. It relates to the position at which, in some species, new leaves regularly develop on branches, and it also appears in the formation of the sunflower florets' spirals. Its value is 137.5° and can be determined by dividing the circumference *c* of a circle into two uneven sections *a* and *b*, where *a* is smaller than *b* and *b:a=c:b* (Fig. 1.16).

The two pictures in figure 1.18

▲ *1.12 – Golden rectangle hosts four golden spirals*

▶ *1.13 – The golden flower stretches between Infinities. It originates from a triangle which mirrors itself while it goes through endless cycles of diminution and augmentation ruled by Φ.*

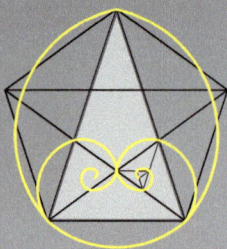

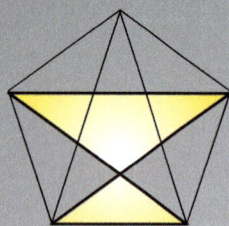

GOLDEN PROPORTION

▲ *1.14 – Two golden spirals in a golden triangle*

▲ *1.15 – The golden bowl*

In order to ENTER the rotational-female-matter, linear-masculine-energy must be initiated in the spiral dance path of momentum.

The path of conservation of momentum between frequencies on the (t) light rope between energy and matter, line and circle, is the GOLDEN MEAN SPIRAL.

Daniel Winter

b

222.5°

137.5°

a

$$c = a + b$$

$$\frac{b}{a} = \frac{c}{b} = \Phi$$

$$\frac{222.5}{137.5} = \frac{360}{222.5} = \Phi$$

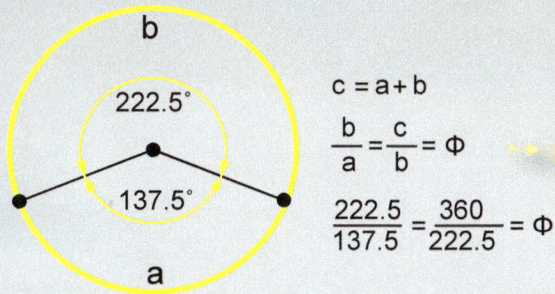

◄ *1.17 – The golden circle*

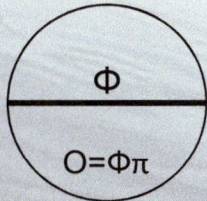

Φ

$$O = \Phi\pi$$

feature the *golden proportion* within a circle: first with an equilateral triangle inscribed inside it, and second with a square inscribed in one half of a circle.

The *golden circle* is a circle the diameter of which is Φ (Fig. 1.17). Its circumference is therefore Φ times π (C=Φπ). With the presence of two *irrational numbers*, this circle in particular reminds us of the ineffable nature of the Source.

Like agents between the metaphysical and the physical, π and Φ work as two sacred secrets of Creation – which symbolically began with a sphere, as feminine. Since everything emerged from a sphere, everything is feminine in its essence. Transformation into masculine is provided later. The curve is older than the straight line.

The spiral is an open circle hurrying to infinity. Φ is the code of such a perfect advancement, epitomised in the *golden spiral*.

GEOMETRIC AND ARITHMETIC PROPORTION IN ONE

As a mathematical discipline, arithmetic can provide an explanation of the tangible physical world however so far, even with all its tools, it was not able to define any spiritual phenomena. On the other hand, the visual vocabulary of geometry is convenient for picturing even the numbers with irrational values and therefore to describe rationally inexplicable notions.

The *arithmetic proportion* appears when a quality is changed by addition, while a change in *geometric proportion* is achieved through multiplication. Since Φ can figure in both *arithmetic* and *geometric proportions*, it might be seen as a bridging element between the worlds of matter and Spirit. How can it exist in both of these proportions? We will refer to figure 1.19 to explain this.

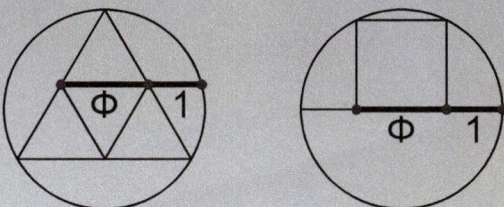

Φ 1

Φ 1

▲ *1.18 – The golden proportion within a circle*

By rotating the long side (A) of the smallest *golden rectangle* (1xA), 90 degrees around one of its end points, we create the long side of a new *golden rectangle* (B). If the shorter side of the starting *golden rectangle* is one unit long (1), then its longer side is Φ times longer, which is just Φ (1xΦ=Φ, A=Φ). On the other side, the newly created *golden rectangle* has sides with the following values: the shorter side A=Φ, and the longer side B=ΦxΦ (B=Φ²) because it is Φ times longer than the short one. The value of B is described through *geometric proportion*. Interestingly, the same *golden rectangle* also contains an *arithmetic proportion* based on Φ. The value of its shorter side (A) is Φ, while the value of its longer side (B), which equals the sum of the two sides of the initial *golden rectangle*, (1+A), can also be shown to be 1+Φ. The value 1+Φ and value ΦxΦ relate to the same length (B), therefore: 1+Φ=ΦxΦ. This equation brings together *arithmetic* and *geometric proportions* generated through Φ. The trajectory of the swinging arms, that create a succession of growing *golden rectangles*, marks a *golden spiral*.

To further clarify this unique property of Φ, let us observe two number series:

A) *Φ-series* obtained through addition:
0.618, 1, 1.618, 2.618, 4.236, 6.854, 11.090…

B) *Φ-series* obtained through the power of Φ:
1.618 (Φ^1); 2.618 (Φ^2); 4.236 (Φ^3); 6.854 (Φ^4); 11.090 (Φ^5)…

And, let us compare the terms of these two series:

$$0{,}618 = \Phi^{-1}$$
$$1 = \Phi^0$$
$$1{,}618 = 1+0{,}618 = \Phi^1$$
$$2{,}618 = 1{,}618+1 = \Phi^2$$
$$4{,}236 = 2{,}618+1{,}618 = \Phi^3$$
$$6{,}854 = 4{,}236+2{,}618 = \Phi^4$$
$$11{,}090 = 6{,}854+4{,}236 = \Phi^5$$

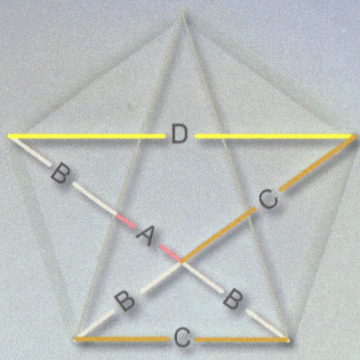

It is evident that both series are made of the same numbers yet they are generated in a different way: A) by adding two previous terms and B) by calculating an adequate power of Φ. For example, in the series A the number 4.236 is obtained by adding two previous consecutive terms (1.618+2.618=4.236) whereas in the series B by calculating Φ to the power of 3 (Φ^3=4.236).

$$A/1 = \Phi$$
$$B/A = \Phi$$
$$C/B = \Phi$$
$$D/C = \Phi$$
$$\Phi = 1{,}618$$

$$A = 1\times\Phi = \Phi$$
$$B = 1 + A = 1 + \Phi$$
$$B = A\times\Phi = \Phi\times\Phi$$

$$1+\Phi = \Phi\times\Phi$$

1.19 – The observation of Φ in a golden rectangle and in a regular pentagon/pentagram

▼ 1.20 – *The ideal self-similarity of measures and shapes as a result of simultaneous adding and multiplying enabled through the golden proportion.*

Φ (1.618…) is a most constructive ratio. It secures harmonious and infinite coexistence on a path of perfect compression/decompression.

Golden Ratio based SELF-SIMILARITY is the ELECTRICAL CAUSE of GRAVITY. – Daniel Winter

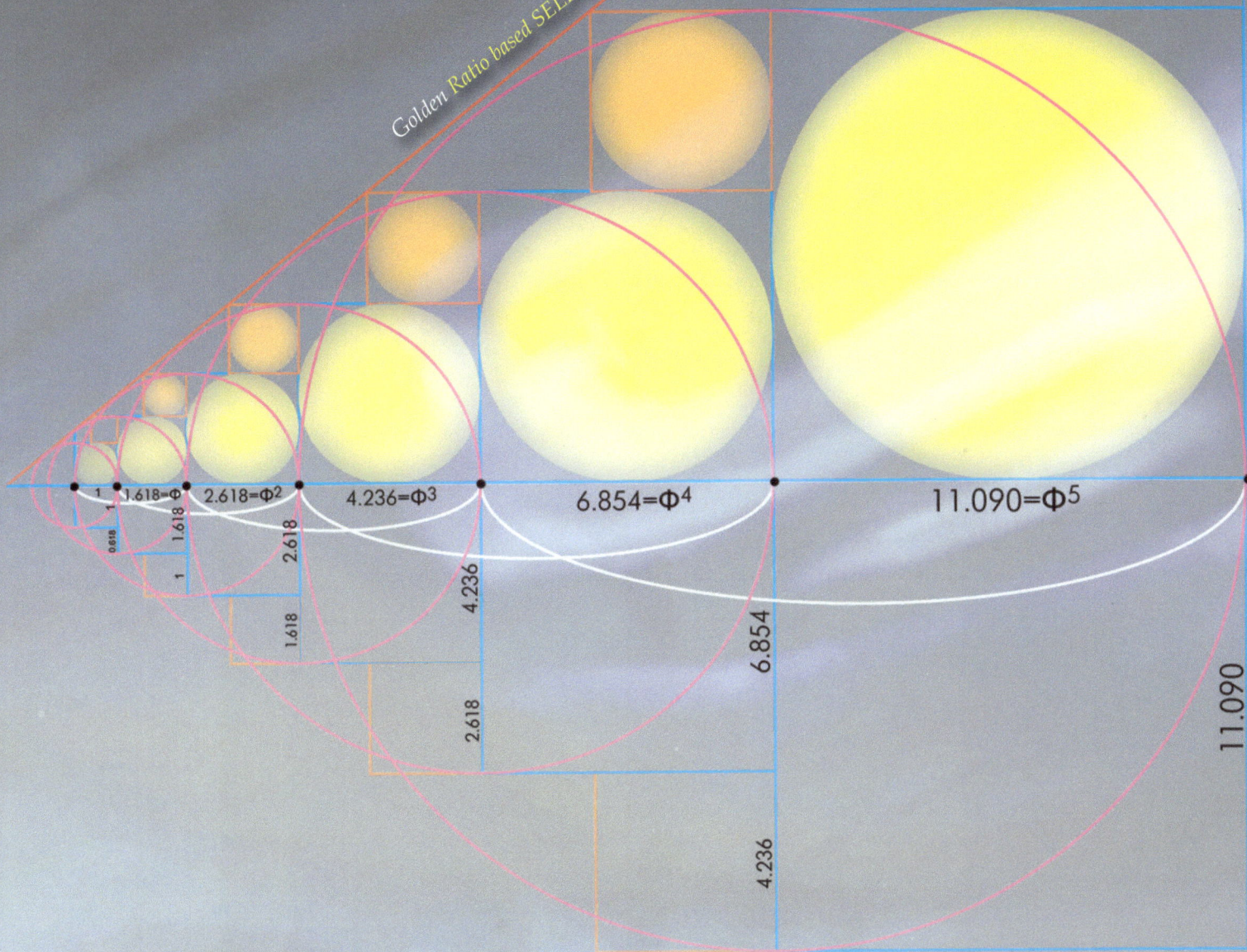

1 $1.618 = \Phi$ $2.618 = \Phi^2$ $4.236 = \Phi^3$ $6.854 = \Phi^4$ $11.090 = \Phi^5$

0.618   1   1   1.618   2.618   4.236   2.618   1.618   6.854   4.236   11.090

HOLDING A MEMORY OF THE WHOLE

Beauty and harmony are inseparable. Every harmony has its intrinsic order. The *golden proportion* is the universal key to an order of high integrity. Connecting the uneven parts, it holds a memory of the whole and like a secret energy line stretches through Creation, all the way to the Source. The *golden proportion* is a harmony-scale of Creation.

In *The Bible*, in John 14:9, *Jesus* says: *Anyone who has seen me has seen the Father.* In this expression *Anyone (son of man)* to *Me (Jesus – Son of God)* is as *Jesus (Son of God)* to *Father (God – One, Whole)*. Between the *son of man (a)*, *Jesus* – who is a *Son of God (b)* and *God* – who is the *Father (a+b)*, we can envisage Φ, as a sacred constant, connecting the constituents of this *Holy Trinity*. In the Kabalistic tradition, the relationship between *Moses* and *God* was seen as the relationship between the *Jewish people* and *Moses*, and that triune communication was understood as the *golden proportion*.

From this observation, we see how One acts through Two while Two activates a trinity when relating to the One. In other words, One that becomes Two returns to itself through the function of Three. The trinity is a code of the divine union.

To activate that code inside us, to become an integrated human being after exploring duality and fragmenting the self through ego, one needs to harmonise with the divine waves of God's love-information. They reach the *son of man* through his mature heart and correct thought.

The son of man thus discovers the path paved with the sweetest vibrations of God that remind him of the true nature of BEING. *I am that I am* whispers through vibrations of bliss.

The research of the Russian scientist **Dr Korotkov**[I-5] reveals a *golden proportion*–based electrical pattern of the performance of the heart and the brain when in a state of bliss. So, science confirms that bliss travels on the waves of the *golden proportion*.

We are the parts of the Whole which are to echo its values. Only through the existence of particles is the whole meaningful and can it realise its own purpose. By educating these particles to appreciate it, the whole preserves its own integrity.

The Whole is present in the essence of the human being. To reach the divine light of our essence, means to reach the Whole.

All the seeds, which have been sown in Your Subconscious since Your first existence until today, have prepared You for a certain Medium of Consciousness.

Each seed in the Subconscious blossoms to give its fruits when it meets the Light of Knowledge which carries its own Vibration. Otherwise, it remains fruitless.

Knowledge coming from Billions of Light years is hidden in Your Brain Layers. That means, each of You is a walking Library. However, You read only the Book You open. This occurs by a process Your Curiosity Code performs.

First, Curiosity drives You into a Medium of Quest. You search first Unawarely, then in Awareness until You find the equivalent of the Frequency You possess.

You know that the speed of Thought is equal to the speed of Light in zero World Frequency. You begin to get Information from the Medium of whichever Dimension Your Thoughts enter.

In more advanced Dimensions, Your speed of Thought transcends the speed of Light. And We have to Inform you that none of these procedures are easy at all.

The Knowledge Book (F5, p 65, par 2-7)[I-6]

GOLDEN PROPORTION

Starting with one pair of rabbits and supposing they produce a new pair of rabbits in their second month, and a new pair of rabbits in every month thereafter, assuming the new rabbits do exactly the same, how many pairs of rabbits will there be in ten months if all of them survive?

The solution to this problem, which **Leonardo Fibonacci** set out to find, led to the discovery of a number series which today bears his name – the *Fibonacci series*.

Fibonacci was the nickname of an Italian (**Leonardo de Pisa**, 1170–1250), who lived in North Africa where he learned Arabic sciences from books such as those of **Al Khwarizmi** (790-840), one of the greatest Arabian mathematicians from the area of the present-day Iraq. With his work *The book of the abacus (Liber abaci)*, **Fibonacci** contributed towards the introduction of Zero, 0, and Arabic numerals to Europe. In the same writing, he also defined a series of numbers later named after him – though it is not quite certain if he understood the connection between the *golden proportion (Φ)* and his number series.

The *Fibonacci series* is a sequence of numbers which starts with Zero and where each number equals the sum of the two previous ones. This means that the sum of any two consecutive numbers produces the next number in the series. For example, 8 and 13 generate the next term (21) through their sum (8+13).

The numbers in this series are often called *Fibonacci numbers*. There are a few *figurate numbers* within them: the numbers 1, 3, 21, 55 – the only *triangular Fibonacci numbers,* and 1 and 144 – the only *square Fibonacci numbers.*

◀ *1.21 – Decomposition with a memory of the whole*

0, 1, 1, 2, 3, 5, 8, 13, 21, 34, 55, 89, 144...

The Australian **Jain** studied the *Fibonacci series* by reducing its numbers to their digital root and discovered a pattern in which numbers appear. *Digital roots of every 24 consecutive numbers of the Fibonacci series* produce a series of digits which repeats itself in every following group of 24 *Fibonacci numbers* and so on *ad infinitum*. Seen this way, the *Fibonacci series* is a series of the following 24 digits that constantly repeat:

1,1,2,3,5,8,4,3,7,1,8,9,8,8,7,6,4,1,5,6,2,8,1,9

Below the group of the first 12 digits, **Jain** placed the group of the second 12 digits of this 24-digit series and aligned them vertically:

1, 1, 2, 3, 5, 8, 4, 3, 7, 1, 8, 9
8, 8, 7, 6, 4, 1, 5, 6, 2, 8, 1, 9

To **Jain**, this is the Φ-code where each of the 12 vertical pairs adds up to 9, or 9 is the *digital root* of their sum.
These 12 times 9 (12x9) produce 108 – the number revered as sacred in Hinduism.

We can determine any n^{th} number in the *Fibonacci series* by the formula:

$$F_n = 1/\sqrt{5}\{[(1 + \sqrt{5})/2]^n - [(1 - \sqrt{5})/2]^n\} \text{ or}$$
$$F_n = [\Phi^n - (-\varphi)^n]/\sqrt{5}, \quad \Phi=1,618... \quad \varphi=0,618...$$

If we take the ratio of every two consecutive *Fibonacci numbers* from the beginning of the series we shall have:

1 / 0
1 / 1 = 1
2 / 1 = 2
3 / 2 = 1.500
5 / 3 = 1.666
8 / 5 = 1.600
13 / 8 = 1.625
21 / 13 = 1.615
34 / 21 = 1.619
55 / 34 = 1.618
89 / 55 = 1.618...
... *ad infinitum.*

We see that the ratio of each two successive numbers quickly converges to Φ. Since the *Fibonacci series* approximates Φ, by becoming infinitely close to Φ, it is asymptotically equivalent to the *Φ-series*. On the other hand, the ratio of consecutive numbers in the *Φ-series* constantly equals Φ.

There are other sequences, beside *Fibonacci series*, in which the ratio of their successive numbers, after some steps, approximates Φ. These are the additive series that begin with two ascending numbers, like for example the series 3, 4, 7, 11, 18, 29, 47, 76, 123,... *ad infinitum*.

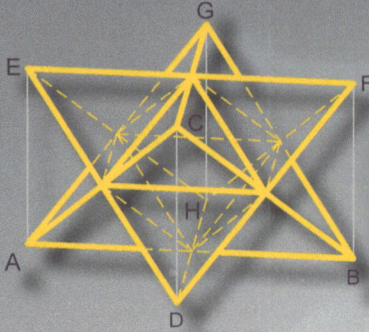

$$4 / 3 = 1.333$$
$$7 / 4 = 1.750$$
$$11 / 7 = 1.571$$
$$18 / 11 = 1.636$$
$$29 / 18 = 1.611$$
$$47 / 29 = 1.621$$
$$76 / 47 = 1.617$$
$$123 / 76 = 1.618... ad\ infinitum.$$

▲ 1.22 – *Jain considers the 24 recurring digits of the Fibonacci series a base of the Φ-code. To him, the star-tetrahedron, with its 24 faces (and 24 edges), is an ideal host to the 24 digits of the Φ-code.*

▼ 1.23 - *Following Jain's view, we can place 24 digits of the Φ-code (12 pairs), onto the 24 faces of the start-tetrahedron so that the sum (or its digital root) of each two digits on the opposing faces is 9.*

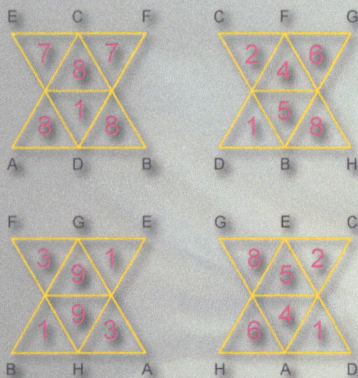

The *Fibonacci series* begins with *Zero* that symbolises the Great Void. The next number is *One*, the *Monad*. So the Great Void brings the *Monad* into existence. Together, they make a unity of a new quality, a new whole. Adding the two latest numbers in the series produces the next number, providing growth through the principle of self-accumulation, as a growth from within which takes nothing from the outside. It is a self-sustainable progression based on the full utilisation of its immediate past. This phenomenon is noticeable in the growth of human body, and in plant and animal growth. The *golden number Φ,* which the *Fibonacci series* tends to generate, perfectly demonstrates the inclusiveness that God operates with.

(Is it mere coincidence that the external angles of the Pentacle are 108 degrees!) It means that the frequency of 108 is the hidden pulse, or rhythm that is the essence of the living mathematics of Nature – it is the reason why the Vedas worshiped this number by incorporating it into their 108 rosary beads when they chant their most famous of all mantras, the Gayatri mantra. It is the most famous Eastern song or Prayer of Enlightenment which is always chanted 108 times, and also has a rhythm of 24 syllables!

Jain

▶ 1.24 – *Harmonic growth through the square root of 2*

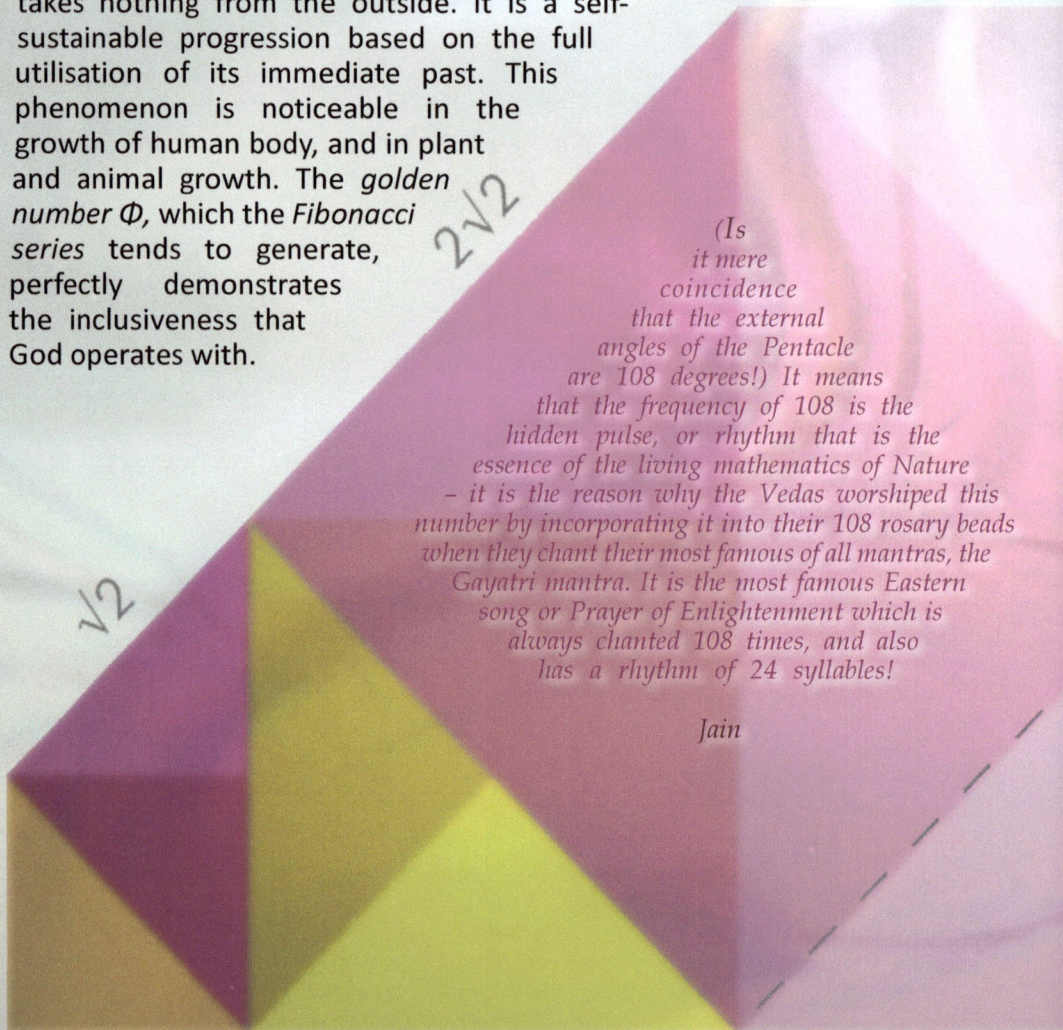

GOLDEN PROPORTION

The primal division fashioned by Φ is asymmetrical. It is not one of the ratio *a:a*. In division based on the *golden proportion,* there is a difference but not equality between the terms. This difference is the catalytic force that enables the dynamics, rhythm and growth. Sameness is static by its nature and does not initiate change.

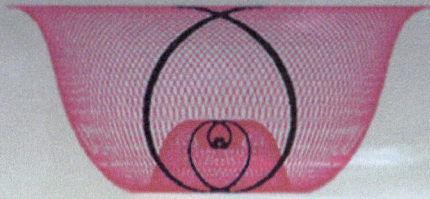

▲ *1.25 – Is this golden cup a REAL GRAIL? – wonders* **Daniel Winter** *(illustration by Daniel Winter)*

The fire of life itself lays in the symmetry Operations Which make this Self-organising IMPLOSION Self-sustainable.

Daniel Winter

Growth through the *golden proportion* is guided from within, which is illustrated in figure 1.19 with an example of the *golden rectangle*'s progression. However, if the progression is generated by the square root of 2, growth is made in a rather different way by being the result of only a partial utilisation of existing values through a new form (Fig. 1.24). Our body also employs the principle of growth based on the square root of 2.

PRINCIPLE OF CREATION IS THE COMPRESSION OF CHARGE

The ability of Φ to provide for both *arithmetic* and *geometric progression* is the key factor in the sustainability of the life of waves. According to one of the latest cosmological theories, *All That Is* is a unified field made of waves. In constant flux, the waves which meet need to agree on coexistence and adopt a pattern that provides for it. That pattern requires a simultaneous addition and multiplication in order for waves to continue living. When no concordant solution between them is found, unconstructive interference leads them into self-destruction.

Only the *golden proportion* provides a way for simultaneous and endless adding and multiplying (Fig. 1.20). As waves of electrical charge adopt that pattern, they start packing themselves in fractals and thus compress. This compression causes acceleration. Acceleration creates gravity, which sucks in the charge or implosion. In the compression of the charge, inertia appears and, at that point, energy turns into matter or mass – as **Daniel Winter** explains. He considers matter to be a result of a particular squeezing of energy and believes that with the help of our heart we can learn to create matter, since *the principle of creation is the compression of charge.* **Winter** also points out that: *only shareable waves, which can agree and get in phase, survive* and that *the role of mind among the waves is to teach them to agree.* This agreement of waves, he calls *coherence* or *pure intention.*

Life IS where the MOST WAVES TOUCH! (Harmonic Inclusiveness predicts vitality in everything that lives). LIFE itself is another way of talking about the infinite communication based on the golden mean that happens between waves when they compress perfectly into IMPLOSION/FUSION.

Your blood becomes powerful and gravity making ('star inhabiting' and 'sun god' making) when it has the opportunity to implode with charge in presence of Bliss.

The solution to get the blood charged with the true physics of Bliss process may actually be the REAL GRAIL.

Daniel Winter

4√2

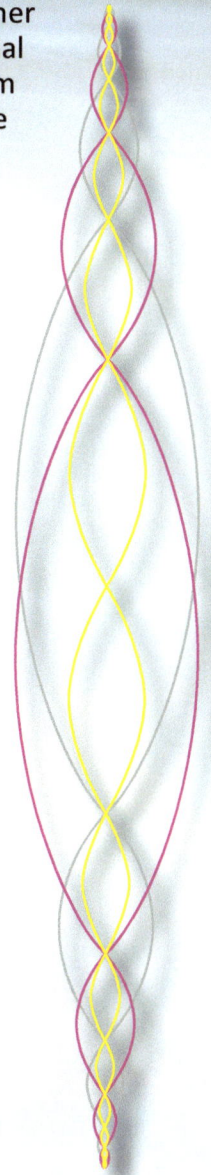

▲ *1.26 – Φ-waves know how to agree and travel together to infinity*

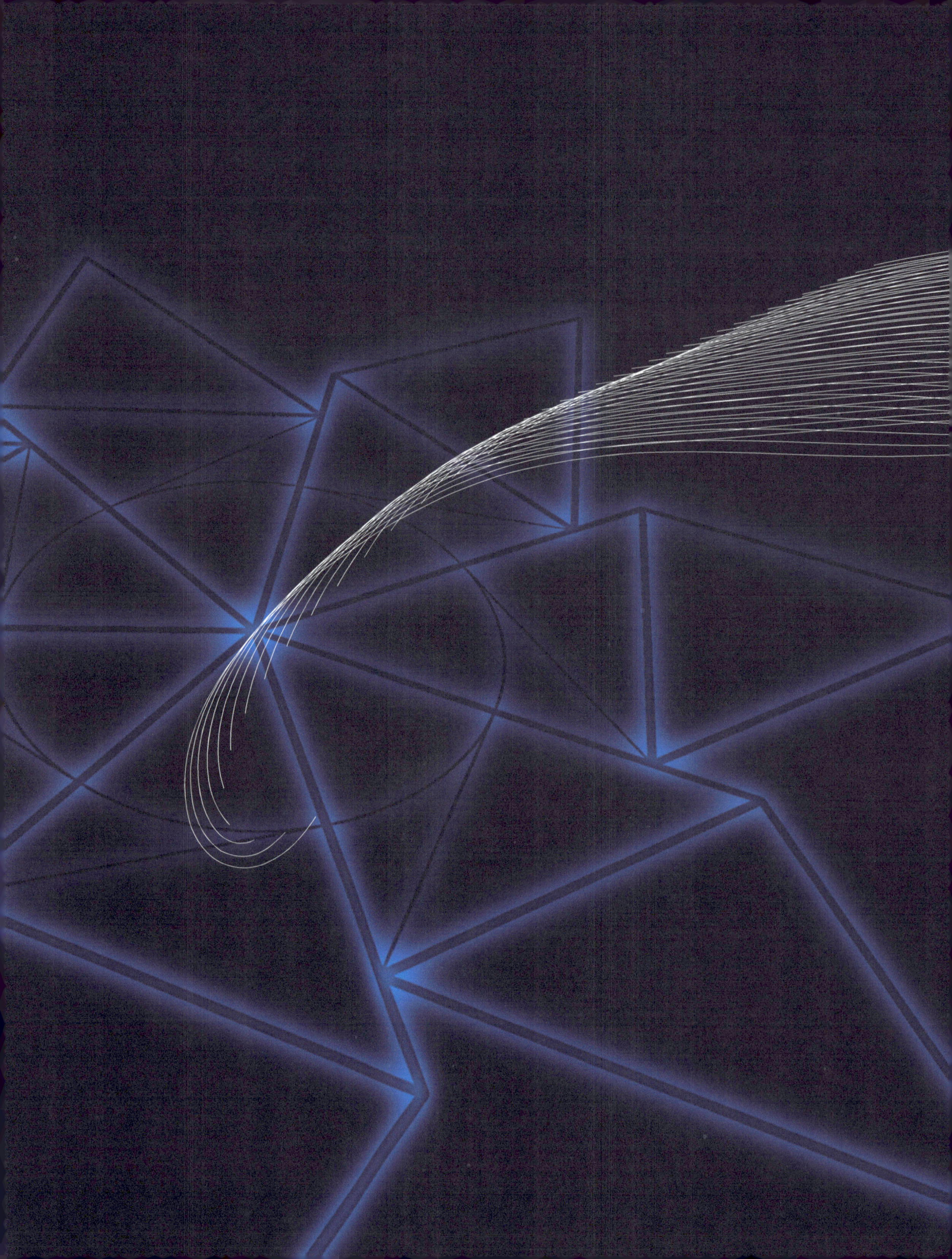

GOLDEN PROPORTION MANIFESTED

FROM UNIVERSE TO ATOM

THE UNIVERSE AND OUR SOLAR SYSTEM

The *golden proportion,* expressed through the mathematical constant Φ (1.618...), is the most refined proportion present in both visible and invisible worlds. It can be found in all levels of Creation, from the tiniest structures of atoms and molecules to the relationships between celestial bodies.

Science indicates that our universe is in the shape of a dodecahedron, which is one of *the Platonic solids* made of twelve regular pentagons. Since the geometry of the regular pentagon is based on the *golden proportion* (Fig. 1.9, 1.19), the design of the whole universe is determined by the sacred constant Φ. The geometry of the zodiac and Earth's grid can also be reduced to pentagonal patterns, in which Φ is the key element of the energy configuration.

In our solar system, distances between planets, as well as those between the planets and the Sun, are all linked to *golden number Φ.*

From figure 2.1 we can see that the Moon fits into a square the sides of which are three units, and the Earth into a square with sides of eleven units. We can also notice that the relationship between the Earth and the Moon is expressed through the geometry of *squaring the circle*. Furthermore, their distance in miles can also be represented as the multiplication of the Earth's radius by 60: 3960x60=237600 (from the triangle 3-4-5: 3x4x5=60). This result is accurate with a less than 0.2% margin of error. Another interesting calculation can be made using this illustration and it will show with 99.96% precision that the sum of Earth's and Moon's circumferences is equal to the perimeter of the square drawn around the Earth:

$$(7920+2160)\pi =$$
$$10080 \times 3.14159 = 31667$$
$$7920 \times 4 = 31680$$

The number 144, which is a number in the *Fibonacci series,* figures as a common denominator in the diameters of the Sun, the Moon and the Earth. The same drawing reveals certain cosmological connotations of the *Great Pyramid* in Egypt, connecting its proportions with those of celestial bodies.

GREAT PYRAMID

An unusual property of the *Great Pyramid*'s design is in the presence of three mathematical constants in its geometry: the *irrational numbers* Φ, π and $e^{(\pi-1)}$. We shall focus on Φ and π because it is easier to observe the way they are employed. Before we begin, it is necessary to mention that the major measures of this monument, expressed in whole numbers of the ancient Egyptian unit called a *Thoth cubit* or *royal cubit,* for practical reasons in

All the Universal Totalities are an Atomic Whole constituted of Triangles within Triangles, Prisms within Prisms.

Everything in the Universe consists of the projectors within a Prismal Order. Light speeds are projected from Universe to Universe by this means. The secret of the Universe is the secret of the Pyramids. And each Human Being is a Natural Pyramid. For this reason the Human being is a Secret of The Universe.

Each Human Being has Special Magnetic Fields peculiar to himself/herself. The entire body is constituted of Triangles of a Unified Field.

.

The Knowledge Book
(F52, p 902, par 9,10;
p 903, par 1)

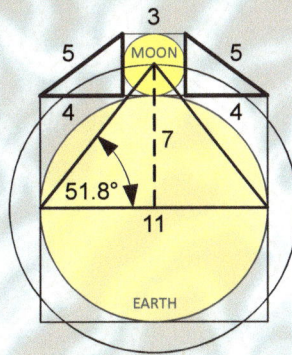

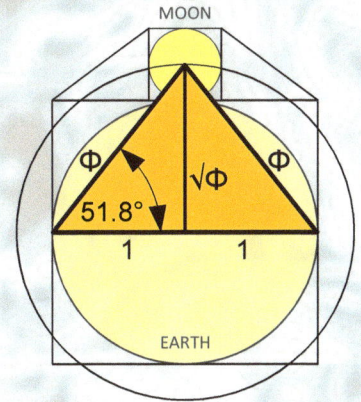

MOON	EARTH	SUN
D	D	D
2160	7920	864000
15x**144**	55x**144**	6000x**144**

(144 – number in the
Fibonacci series,
D – diameter in miles)

▲ 2.1 – *Some arithmetical and
geometrical relations of Earth,
Moon and Sun*

▲ 2.2 – *The geometry of the
Great Pyramid keeps a record
of the Earth-Moon relationship
based on Φ*

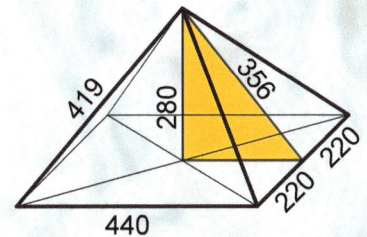

▲ 2.3 – *The Great Pyramid's
measurements expressed in an
ancient Egyptian measuring
unit called the royal cubit*

the following analyses will often have their values reduced by a factor of ten so that 440 becomes 44, 280 becomes 28, 1760 becomes 176, and so on in a given observation.

From figure 2.3 we can calculate:
$$2 \times 440/280 = 880/280 = 22/7 = 3.143 \sim \pi$$
$$356/220 = 1.618 \sim \Phi$$

The fraction 22/7 (3.14286...) is the closest value of π that can be expressed with whole numbers, while 28/22 stands for the square root of Φ ($\sqrt{\Phi}=1.27273...$). Starting from these equations we can ascertain what the ancient Egyptians, through their most famous architectural work, have been telling us about the π and Φ relationship.

$$22/7 \sim \pi \qquad \rightarrow \qquad 22 = 7\pi$$
$$28/22 \sim \sqrt{\Phi} \qquad \rightarrow \qquad 22 = 28/\sqrt{\Phi}$$
$$7\pi = 28/\sqrt{\Phi} \qquad \rightarrow \qquad \pi = 4/\sqrt{\Phi} \qquad \sqrt{\Phi} = 4/\pi$$

This simple analysis shows how the *master number* 22 connects π and Φ. The number 176 is also relevant to this building. It can be represented as: 11+11+22+44+88=176.

All these *master numbers* (11, 22, 44 and 88) appear in various measurements of the *Great Pyramid*, albeit only when the *royal cubit* is used as the measuring unit (Fig. 2.7).

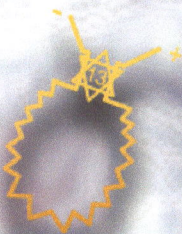

The most intimate relationship between π and Φ is revealed through the measure of a *royal cubit* since the *royal cubit* can be defined through either π or Φ. Results obtained from calculations based on these *irrational numbers* provide almost identical values for a *royal cubit*.

One sixth of π gives 0.523599:
$\pi/6 = 3.141592/6 = 0.523599$

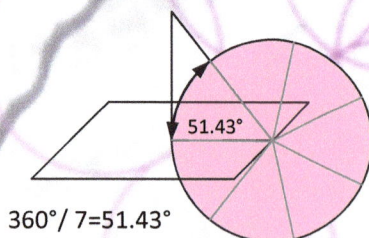

▶ *2.4 – The triangle of the Great Pyramid's slope*

while one fifth of Φ squared equals 0.523607:
$\Phi^2/5 = 1.618034^2/5 = 2.618034/5 = 0.523607$.

These values give the *royal cubit* definition in metres, and the difference of 0.000008m (0.0008cm) indicates that the ancient Egyptian builders based their measuring system of the *Great Pyramid* on a unit that merged π and Φ with an astonishing accuracy. Being derived from two *irrational numbers*, the *royal cubit* itself is a close relative of *irrational numbers* and could be seen as a member of the same family. It brings together two constants which translate the divine perfection of the circle (π) and the *golden spiral* (Φ) into the tangible world. The ancient Egyptians literally made π and Φ visible by building this monument of eternity, and for eternity. They impregnated it with sacred mathematical constants thus securing harmonies of the highest cosmic order in its form.

Looking at the numbers significant in the *Great Pyramid*'s design, we can notice that the numbers 28 and 7 are amongst them. As we have seen in the book *All is Number (Number Six; Number Seven)*, 28 is what we call a *perfect number* – while the number Seven itself holds the memory of infinity. Both of these numbers are significant in the measuring system based on the *royal cubit*. A seventh of a *royal cubit* is called a *palm* which is 7.48cm, while a quarter of a *palm* is known as a *finger* (1.87cm). The *royal cubit* therefore has 28 *fingers* and equals 52.36cm. The number 28 is also a *triangular number* because it can be represented in the form of a triangle. We could demonstrate it with seven rows of pebbles where each row has one pebble more than the previous one: 1, 2, 3, 4, 5, 6, 7.

When you understand the relationship of the Orthogonal reality to the golden proportion you will uncover the illusion of linear time.

The Group[(II-2)] *through Steve Rother*

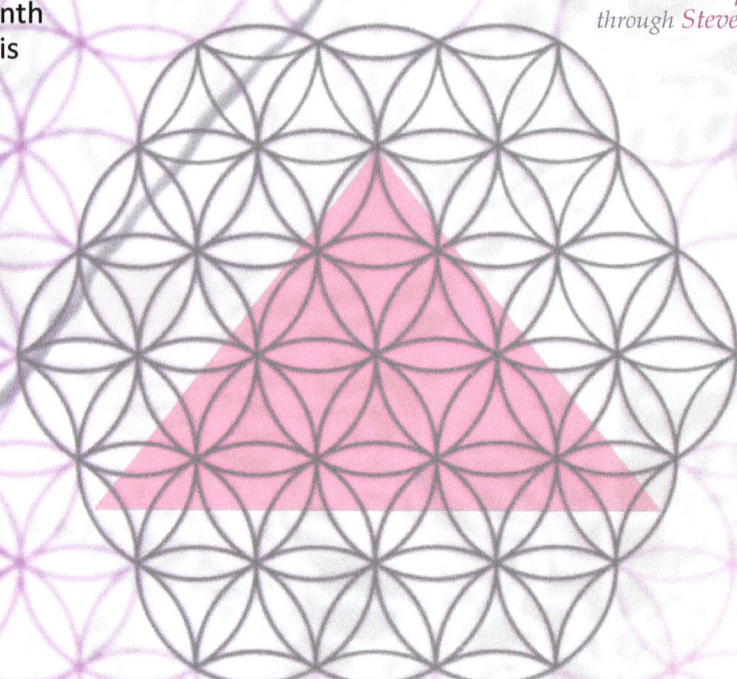

▲ *2.5 – The Great Pyramid and the flower of life*

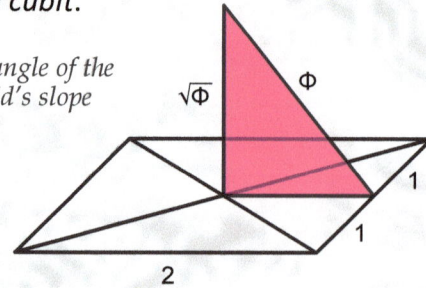

360°/ 7=51.43°

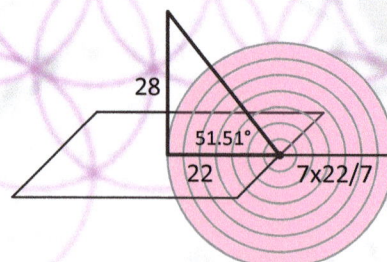

◀ *2.6 – Seven in relation to the full circle and the Great Pyramid (π~22/7)*

Another appearance of Seven is related to π. The numerical value reduced by a factor 10, of the half length of the *Pyramid*'s side, divided by Seven gives π (22/7=3.143... ~ π). When 28 and 22 are related to define the angle of the *Pyramid*'s slope, through the formula tan⁻¹(28/22), they give an angle of 51.84° (51°51'). Interestingly, one seventh of the full circle corresponds to that angle with a 99.96% accuracy (360°/7=51.43°), (Fig. 2.6).

The numerical concurrences that are encountered when analysing the *Great Pyramid* make it evident that we are dealing with a masterpiece from beyondness; with a tangible eternity that landed in the fertile valley of the Nile some 45 centuries ago, at least. It might well be a giant planetary tuning fork, or musical instrument, emanating sublime celestial vibrations and passing to us a message of some unchanging order from higher worlds. Or, does the *Great Pyramid* equally work as a sprinkler of cosmic influences that stabilise and enhance our physical reality and help us evolve faster?

GREAT PYRAMID AND SQUARING THE CIRCLE

The *Great Pyramid* at Giza, also gives a practical contribution towards the solution of the *squaring the circle* puzzle (Fig. 2.7). Some of its basic measurements can be used to construct a circle and a square, in which the circumference of the circle and the perimeter of the square are the 'same'. For that purpose, the base of the Pyramid is the square while the radius of the circle, which fits into the criteria of the puzzle, is the height of the Pyramid. The intersection of the base's diagonals is the centre of the circle. According to actual measurements of the *Great Pyramid*, the perimeter of the square is 1760 *royal cubits* and the circumference of the circle produced that way is 1759.3 *royal cubits*.

P = 4 x 440 = 1760 Rc
C = 2 x 280 x π = 1759.3 Rc
C = 1760 Rc
Rc - *Royal cubit*

This method of *squaring the circle* exposes the unusual scope needed to deliver the suitable result. It involves the three-dimensional alignment of some elements that are a particular of this *Pyramid*'s geometry.

The circle that we look for to match the *Pyramid*'s square base, besides involving π, in this case also incorporates Φ.

280   220 220   440

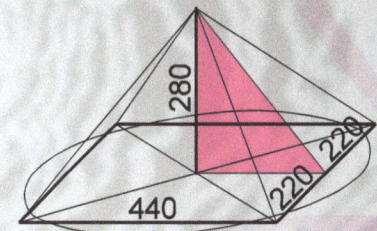

▲ *2.7 – The height of the Great Pyramid is equal to the radius of a circle matching the square-base of the Pyramid, in the manner known as squaring the circle*

That way Φ takes an active role in reconciling a square and a circle as the two archetypal forms that represent the two worlds: Earth and the heavens, matter and Spirit, physical and metaphysical. To do so, Φ descended from the *golden triangle* MOL which defines the *Great Pyramid*'s slope (Fig. 2.4, 2.9). Side MO (√Φ) becomes the radius of the circle, while OL (1) corresponds to half of the square side. What an unexpected origin of the radius of the circle which is in divine harmony with the *Pyramid*'s base!

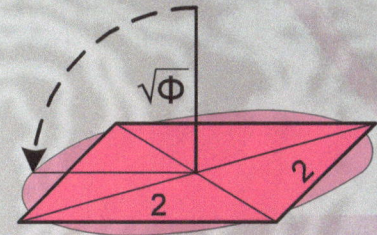

▶ *2.8 – Seven and a circle*

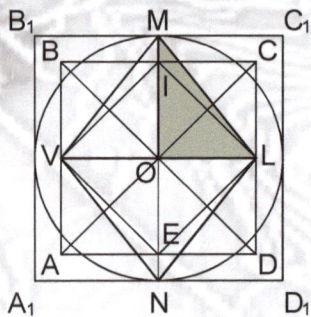

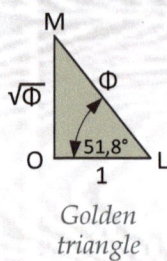

Golden triangle

▲ 2.9 – The Great Pyramid's squaring the circle geometry and the golden triangle of the Pyramid's slope (MOL). This is the only triangle whose sides are in the geometric progression: 1, √Φ, Φ.

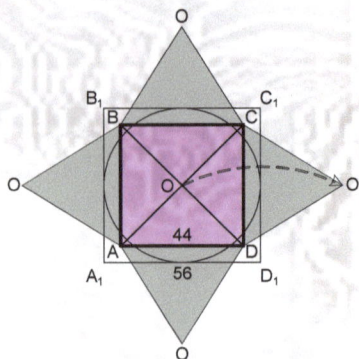

▲ 2.10 – Projecting the sides of the Great Pyramid

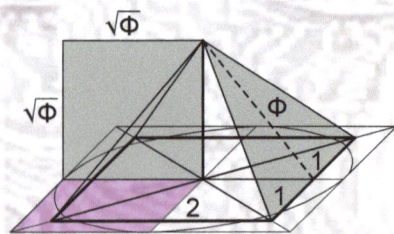

▲ 2.11 – The square of the Great Pyramid's height equals the surface area of one of its sides. The same value is found in one quarter of the surface of the big square ($A_1B_1C_1D_1$) that outlines the circle from the squaring the circle geometry of its base (Fig. 2.9, 2.10).

We see how the triangle MOL of the *Pyramid*'s slope lends two of its sides to the figure of the squared circle and actually completely determines it. This triangle of the *Pyramid* is a very special *golden triangle* (Fig. 2.9). All its sides (1, √Φ, Φ) relate to one another through the *golden proportion*. This is also the only triangle whose sides form the geometrical progression $b^2=ac$ (a=1, b=√Φ, c=Φ; (√Φ)²=1Φ; Φ=Φ).

The unusual concord of the *Great Pyramid*'s shape and measurements extends even further (Fig. 2.10). If we construct a new square ($A_1B_1C_1D_1$) outlining the circle which forms the *squaring the circle* geometry with the *Pyramid*'s base, the surface area of that bigger square is equal to the surface area of the *Pyramid*'s sides composed of four triangles. Thus we have $A_1B_1C_1D_1$=ABO+BCO+CDO+DAO (Fig. 2.10). The knowledge of this equation was passed from the ancient Egyptians to the Greeks by **Herodotus** (484bc-432bc): *The square of the Pyramid's height is equal to the surface area of one of its sides* (Fig. 2.11).

The *golden proportion* echoes throughout the body of the *Great Pyramid* since it is present in numerous ratios of its constructive elements. Looking at figures 2.12 and 1.21, we can realise how an endless number of *golden triangles* can be generated starting from the MOL triangle of the *Great Pyramid*'s slope illustrating the harmonic potential of its form. Φ works as a divine trigger and the carrier of that endless harmony. With the architectural configuration and the ambience of the *Great Pyramid*, for thousands of years Φ has been inviting us to higher realities, or higher states of being, by manifesting a portal to infinity before our very eyes.

Whatever the final answer to the *Great Pyramid* of Giza turns out to be, one truth is already clear: since it was built, the *Great Pyramid* has been serving as an awe and curiosity generator, stretching the human mind from the context of the terrestrial to the cosmic. Endeavours to solve the biggest building enigma on the planet have resulted in numerous researches on the site and a huge number of books being written on the subject. While investigating our past, we have been looking into our future.

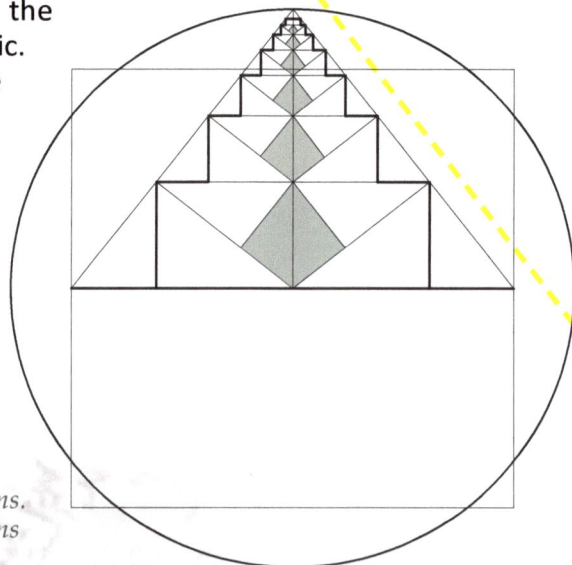

► 2.12 – *The stairway to the heavens. From Earth (square) to the heavens (circle) in Φ-steps.*

Yet, the silent magnificence of this pyramid, as our own secret, seems unreachable. Maybe that is exactly its role: to challenge human beings for the sake of stimulation and the growth of *terrestrial consciousness*. But once we fully understand the function of the pyramid in Creation, as well as that of the triangle and the *irrational numbers Φ, π and e*, we will, most likely, with ease walk out of this dimension of existence where their true significance and potential are still unexplained. Instead of us, ready to wonder about the pyramid, others will come to feed this world's wonder with a new awe and fresh curiosity.

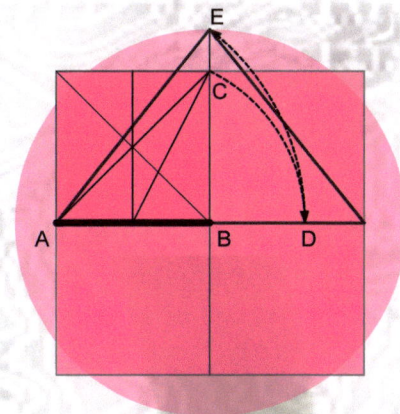

▲ *2.13 – Squaring the circle within the Great Pyramid – the big square is the pyramid base, BE is the radius of the circle required*

The *Great Pyramid* is a monument of our future, yet coming from our planetary past. It has been designed and built by a highly developed culture. However advanced we may look to ourselves, we obviously have not reached the same level of knowledge and consciousness as the ancients so as to be able to fully solve the phenomenon of this exquisite legacy. This is not to say that we have not done well so far, but rather to acknowledge the immensity of the task of becoming greatly evolved and fully conscious human beings.

H^3

R^3

▼ *2.14 – The nest of the Platonic solids, starting from the biggest one, comprises of the: dodecahedron, cube, tetrahedron, octahedron and icosahedron – illustration by Frank van den Bovenkamp (Heart Coherence team)*

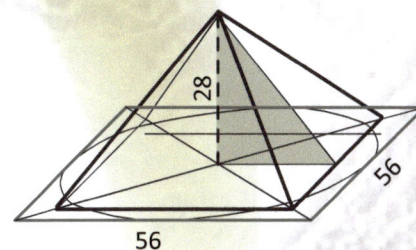

28

56

56

▶ *2.15 – Some measures and geometries related to the Great Pyramid's example of squaring the circle*

The only harmonics to grab wave fronts, going in and out of light speed (black hole), ARE the perfect heterodyning/beating which GOLDEN RATIO permits. This then is literally THE ONLY STAIRWAY TO HEAVEN WHICH EVER EXISTED. It is a discipline of geometry. AND IT DOES HAVE A PSYCHOLOGICAL requirement unequivocally required.

Daniel Winter

NUCLEUS OF AN ATOM

In the book *Messages Behind Shapes*, chapter *One is Many,* we will see how the four *Platonic solids* can nest one inside the other making pairs of the so-called *Platonic duals*: the cube with an octahedron and the icosahedron with a dodecahedron, while the tetrahedron nests into its own form and is considered a dual to itself. The nesting of the *Platonic solids* has an even bigger capacity than what these relationships within the duals reveal.

Actually, dual pairs can also mutually nest. The key question in achieving such a complex symbiosis of forms is how to provide a harmonic connection of two nested pairs. To successfully complete that bridging manoeuvre, each of an octahedron's six vortices needs to touch six, out of twenty, of an icosahedron's faces. The point of contact is at one of the icosahedron's triangular surfaces, and it divides the altitude of that triangle in the *golden proportion*.

We come across the *golden proportion* when the completed nest of the four *Platonic solids* is analysed with the dodecahedron as the outer solid, the icosahedron nested within it containing the octahedron within itself placed in the manner just described, and eventually the cube as an innermost solid. If the edge of the cube is marked as one unit, the proportion between the edge size of the biggest and the smallest solid (dodecahedron-cube) is Φ (Fig. 2.16).

This particular nesting combination of the *Platonic solids* is relevant to the structure of the nucleus of an atom and is the geometrical foundation for periodicity of elements. The template of nested solids (dodecahedron – icosahedron – octahedron – cube) provides the so-called *shells* along which neutrons and protons are spaced. Neutrons occupy the inside of the nucleus and are always one level deeper within the structure than protons. This theory was put forward by the American **Dr Robert J. Moon** (1911-1989), showing on a micro level what four centuries ago **Johannes Kepler** suggested was the principle of harmonies between the celestial bodies of our solar system. The macro order is mirrored on a micro level and the *vice versa*. The same laws govern the entirety of Creation and in the heart of it we find geometries based on the *golden proportion*. It is a ratio that allows the scale of vibrational values to stretch harmoniously and infinitely.

▼ 2.16 – *Edge sizes of the Platonic solids nested in dodecahedron:*

Dodecahedron	1.618
Icosahedron	1.89
Octahedron	2.12
Cube	1

We see how the golden proportion regulates the spatial relationships of the nested Platonic solids (1.618:1)

The structure of the atomic nucleus, as we have just seen, is yet another example of Φ lending, to the tiniest forms of the matter, its unique aptitude to generate and maintain endless harmony. The *golden proportion* regulates the sizes of the nested *Platonic solids*, used by minute particles as a space determinant for their own positioning in creating all known chemical elements. So what might appear like a free and unstructured space in the core of an atom is, geometrically, a very precisely organised environment. It enables a smooth and rhythmical change of qualities and lawful interaction between chemical elements which are the building blocks for all life. The vibrational bonds that hold the atomic particles together are the same bonds that bind the entire universe as a whole. That attraction power is nothing but God's love at work.

▲ 2.17 – *Platonic duals – drawing from Kepler's book Mysterium Cosmographicum*[(II-16)]

GOLDEN PROPORTION MANIFESTED

It has been observed that the division/multiplication of cells after an egg is fertilised, at one point starts showing Φ as a ratio between the numbers of cells in successive phases. However, we can find Φ even at deeper levels of our biological make-up.

Molecules of our DNA are 34 angstroms long and 21 angstroms wide, in each full cycle of their two spiralling strands (double helix), and these numbers are successive numbers in the *Fibonacci series* so their ratio is approximately Φ.

DNA is a long molecule structured into two branches that hold *genetic code triplets*. Alphabetic *triplets* consist of three, out of four, nitrogen bases: A *(adenine)*, C *(cytosine)*, G *(guanine)*, T *(thymine)*. The order in which the bases occur is a genetic code. Branches are linked by nucleotides. Nitrogen bases are arranged in a fashion of complementarity: base A in one branch is always complemented by base T in the other branch and, similarly, base G by base C. If twenty amino acids are encoded using alphabetic triplets, a set of 64 different combinations of *genetic triplets* is obtained. The Russian scientist **Sergei Petoukhov** presented this set of 64 triplets in an 8x8 matrix and called it the *biperiodical table*. He pointed out a great analogy between this system and the Chinese *I Ching* divination system that is also an 8x8 matrix. They both seem to be directed by the same structural principles of natural order.

In 1990, **Jean-Clode Perez** discovered the mathematical rule behind the grouping of the nucleotides in DNA. This rule indicates a high level of self-organisation governed by the *golden proportion* and it is responsible for exhibiting great stability, and yet sufficient sensitivity, in the DNA's structure. In the whole circuit of a DNA molecule, for all combinations of bases, for example A against TCG, the number of A-bases, the number of remaining bases (TCG) and the number of all bases (ATCG) are, or tend to be, three consecutive *Fibonacci numbers*. Any smaller section of DNA is also structured through three adjacent *Fibonacci numbers*. The inherent harmony of the genetic code of DNA based on the *golden proportion,* according to **Perez**, creates a particular 'resonance' and this phenomenon he named the *supra-code* of DNA.

As a result of the high structural order of DNA, its energetic emanations are not a great deal different from those of any other area of life where we find the *Fibonacci series* and the *golden proportion,* be it in music, plants, artwork or architecture. From tiny to galactic structures, we find the *golden proportion* to be a universal organisational principle and a common tool for a perfect function. Smooth functions naturally provide a pleasing aesthetics, thus satisfying our need for beauty.

Scientists discovered that DNA emits a weak form of light. That light is a communication tool of cells and organs of an organism and, as such, is used to establish relations with other organisms. Daniel Winter sees DNA as a perfectly Φ-structured crystal designed to transmit inter-dimensionally, information contained in the light. It is the storage of light in our body and the host of our cellular consciousness.

Light received and emitted through our DNA is an instrument and the language that Spirit uses to operate throughout Creation. Ultimately, that natural language of light might become a soundless language of future humans.

Everything in this Universe is Sacred. While Reality shows itself mostly in the form of chaos and complexity, making up our relative, diverse and unpredictable world, there exists an absolutely sacred order behind and inside all and everything. This has been known since time immemorial as the Sacred Geometry of Creation.

Frank van den Bovenkamp[(II-3)]
(Heart Coherence team)

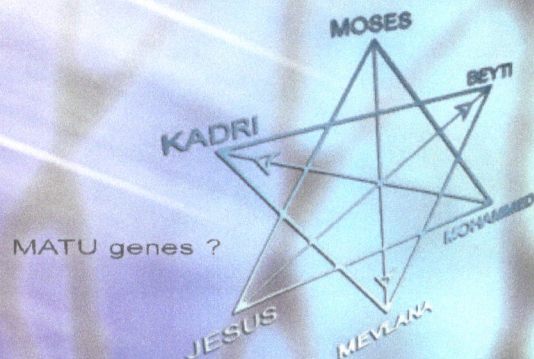

Φ AND THE GEOMETRY OF HUMAN BODY

He created the heavens and the earth in just proportions, and has given you shape, and made your shapes beautiful: and to Him is the final Goal!
The Quran (64:3)

In the geometry of the human body, the *golden proportion* persistently appears. Not only can we divide an ideally proportioned human body into seven Φ sections, but numerous elements of its structure are related through Φ (Fig. 2.19, 2.20). With all these relationships drawn up, the human body looks like a diagram based on the *Fibonacci numbers* and Φ.

When we are born, our navel is positioned exactly in the middle of our height. During puberty, it starts moving towards the point of the *golden proportion* between the parts it identifies, although in an adult female it is slightly higher, and in an adult male it is slightly lower than the Φ point. The navel is the place where the umbilical cord was once attached to the baby's body providing a connection with its mother. This travelling of the navel symbolises our shift in consciousness: from a *dualistic consciousness* of strong polarisation we arrive at *the unity consciousness,* gradually claiming our divine heritage. As the bonding point with the mother-source, the navel divides the height of an adult's body into parts which are approximately related through the *golden proportion*. By linking these parts, Φ secures the perfection of the divine being reflected through the geometry of our body.
On the other hand, the sexual organs of an adult human body are at the body's midpoint, emphasizing that our sexual determiner places our consciousness into a context of two polarised parts. During life, both sexes work on balancing the attributes of the opposite one within. We as souls are One, for at that level we are not attributed with a gender.

Ideally, the diagram of the face is equivalent to the diagram of the body. Also the length of the face is the same as the vertical distance between the navel and the intersection of the legs *(c –* Fig. 2.19). The shorter of the two sections that the navel divides the body's height into (from the navel to the top of the head, *m –* Fig. 2.19) is equal to the vertical distance from the tip of the middle finger (when the arm is hanging down) to the floor.

Many on your world believe that consciousness is anchored in the brain. While your mind is truly prodigious in its abilities, the primary source of your genius, in truth, lies first in your genes, and then your heart. But the pivot to comprehending this is your eternal source – your Soul. This special, infinite collection of Spirit is gifted by the Creator with unique wisdoms. Among them is the ability to discern the real nature of the Universe and the means to manifest the decrees of the divine plan. This potential is invested in the eternal Light and Love that is the real you. This is realized in your genes (the body's greatest Light receptor) and in your heart (your body's greatest accumulator of Love). These divine energies then interact with your spiritual and physical essences to create who you truly are in each of your many lifetimes. From this base and with the help of your physical and emotional essences, you daily encounter and assess your world.

Galactic Federation of Light[II-4]
through Sheldan Nidle

There is much logic in love and that logic was found by the great philosopher Pythagoras and other great mathematicians around the world. There is much to be understood about Sacred Geometry and about energy and how energy flows through your body. The masculine energy and the feminine energy are also based in Sacred Geometry; in fact everything in the universe is based in Sacred Geometry. Where you try and create outside of the boundaries of Sacred Geometry, you are creating something which is not within the Divine will, you are creating something that is negative, something where there is negative flow; this is not to say that your creation is wrong, it is to say that it is a creation creating a negative flow.

Kryon[II-5]
through David Brown

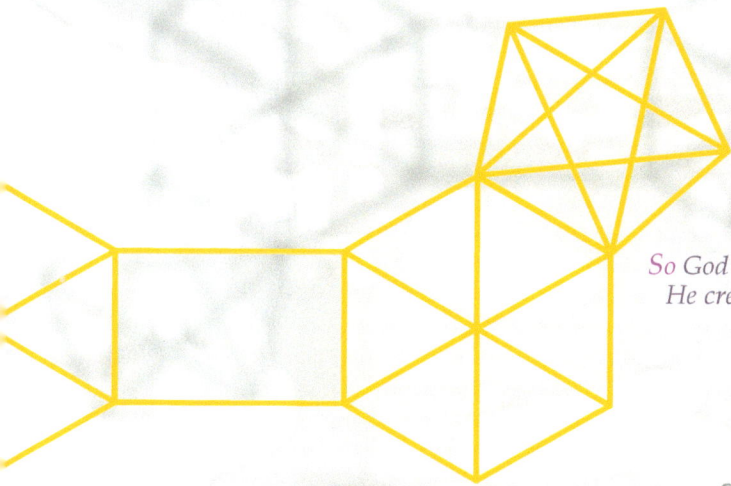

◄ 2.18 – *Our DNA consists of two chains of nucleotides twisted into a double helix. Is the hydrogen bond between these two chains, that connects complementary bases, a golden mean rectangle? – wonders* **Daniel Winter**
(Part of the illustration by **Daniel Winter***)*

So God created man in His own image;
He created him in the image of God.

The Bible
(Genesis 1:27)

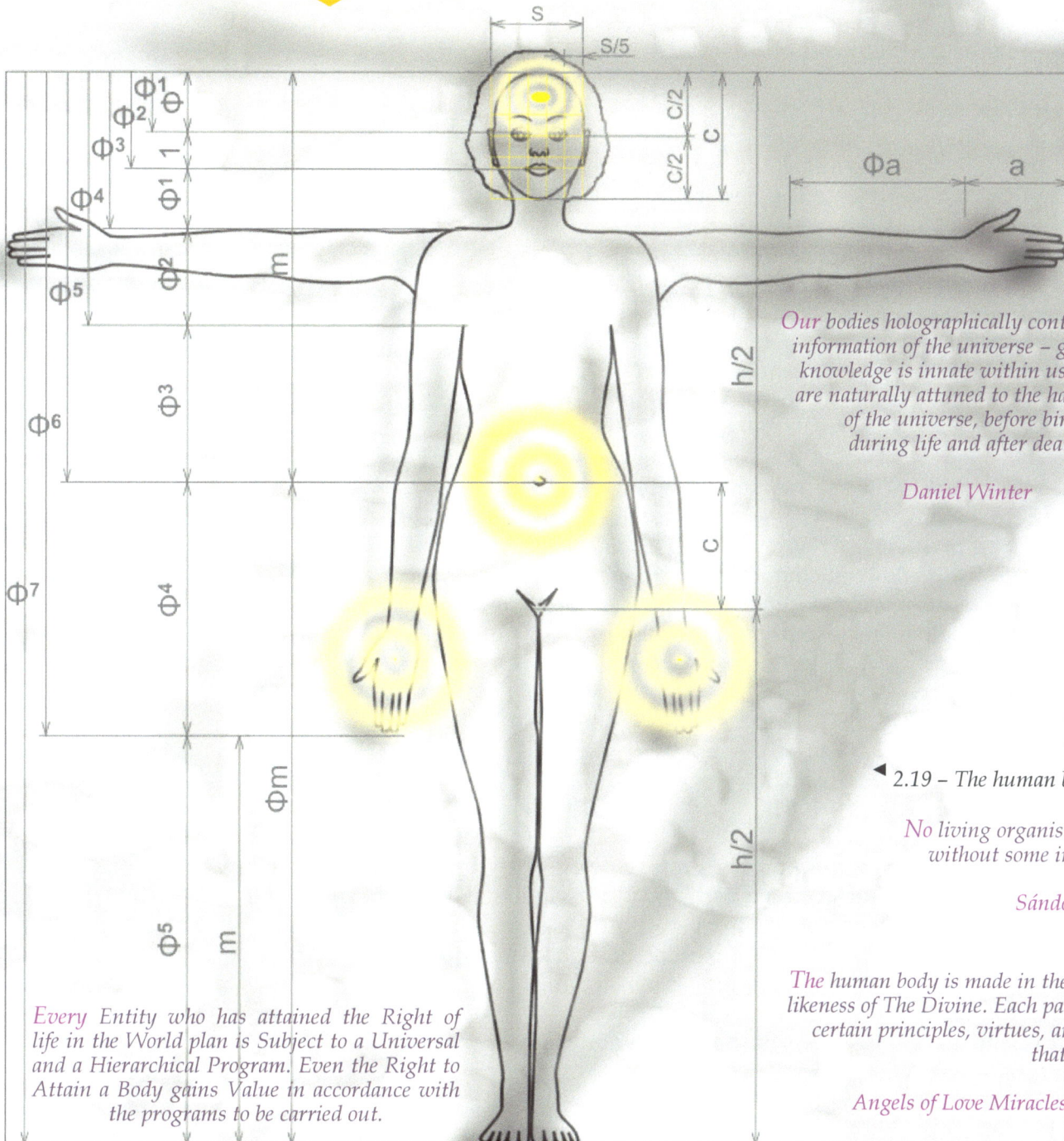

Our bodies holographically contain all the information of the universe – geometric knowledge is innate within us and we are naturally attuned to the harmonics of the universe, before birth, during life and after death.

Daniel Winter

◄ 2.19 – *The human body and* Φ

No living organism is perfect without some imperfection

Sándor Kabai [(II-6)]

The human body is made in the image and likeness of The Divine. Each part embodies certain principles, virtues, and qualities that are divine.

Angels of Love Miracles – Afrei [(II-7)]

Every Entity who has attained the Right of life in the World plan is Subject to a Universal and a Hierarchical Program. Even the Right to Attain a Body gains Value in accordance with the programs to be carried out.

Vedia Bülent (Önsü) Çorak
(Light)

The ratio between the neighbouring bone lengths of our fingers, hands and arms is regulated by the *golden proportion*. This means we can determine the length of the next bigger bone in a finger by multiplying the length of the smaller adjoining one by Φ.

Φ^3

Φ^2

The presence of the *Fibonacci numbers* can be observed in the skeletal structure of the human body and its organs. We have nearly 233 bones, 34 vertebrae, 13 digestive organs, 8 endocrine glands and the base of the palm is composed of 5 bones (metacarpals) each extending into a finger. The numbers that specify the parts of our inner organs are also from the *Fibonacci series:* liver – 8, kidneys – 8, heart – 13, and the respiratory organs also consist of 8 parts.

Scientific researches reveal that many physiological rhythms and functions of inner organs in our body are also regulated by the *golden proportion*. It is detected in respiratory organs, blood pressure and the circulatory system as well as in the functions of the brain, heart and vision. For example, in their book *The golden proportion and a Man*[II-8], **V. I. Korobko** and **G. I. Korobko** point out that the *Fibonacci numbers* mark numerical boundaries of each brain rhythm: *delta:* 1-3, *theta:* 3-8, *alpha:* 8-13, *beta:* 13-34 and *gamma:* 34-55.

The authors also show how the numerical value of the main wave of the *beta* rhythm, which is 21Hz, can be obtained by dividing the whole range of brain biorhythms by Φ^2 (55/2.618=21.01Hz). Similar calculations provide the characteristic frequency range of every brain rhythm, and such evidence unequivocally supports the view of the *golden proportion* being deeply imprinted in the morphology of our being.

BRAIN WAVES

Delta – δ
Pure Being and the Will

Theta – θ
Deep thoughts, deep day dreams, lucid dreaming, hypnotic states, light sleep, states just before falling asleep and waking – all create mental pictures that draw feelings into them.

Alpha – α
Thoughts in a relaxed state, day-dreaming or sleeping states and feelings which attract 3-dimensional material manifestation

Beta – β
State of active awareness, active concentration, logic, busy or anxious thinking, and activities of the five senses experiencing the 3-dimensional world

Gamma – γ
Higher mental activity, interpretation of sensory inputs; and fear

Delta	1+(3-1)/2.618	=	1.76~2Hz	δ
Theta	3+(8-3)/2,618	=	4.91~5Hz	θ
Alpha	8+(13-8)/2.618	=	9.91~10Hz	α
Beta	13+(34-13)/2.618	=	21.02~21Hz	β
Gamma	34+(55-34)/2.618	=	42.02~42Hz	γ

▲ *2.20 – Hand and Φ*

In relation to these findings, the **Korobkos** offer a wider view by disclosing the fact whereby our solar system represents a self-synchronising oscillatory system just like that of the human brain. They point out that the oscillatory character, common to both systems, makes it not accidental that the *golden proportion* regulates the ratio of orbital periods of adjacent planets in the solar system, as well as the ratio of the intervals' boundaries of our brain's biorhythm.

The structure and certain functions of the human body indicate that its principal plan is based upon the *golden proportion*.

However, it is also obvious that life forms only tend to follow that guidance, because life hardly ever complies fully with the laws of the ideal. Specific conditions, in which humans, plants and animals live, cause the deviations from the plan and so contribute to the variety of species and forms in nature.

ON THE ROAD TO ETERNITY

Life-force is the ability to fractally attract and self-organise electrical charge, **Daniel Winter** points out. He explains how the state of bliss, created by the capacity of the heart to generate an implosion in blood DNA, is the moment we create a charge from within. To him, that blissful fire is a *blue light* and a true enlightenment.

The igniting of DNA into bliss, **Daniel Winter** explains through geometry that allows for perfect packing (storing and compressing in a harmonious and shareable manner) in which the waves of charge can become everlasting. For him this is one example of sacredness: *sacred means a pattern which works so well among the waves that it lasts forever.* Thus the *sacred* provides a solution for a harmonious embedment of the life-force which secures a ceaseless flow. Infinite sustainability is a synonym and a secret of immortality.

As beings of an electromagnetic nature, among the unified field of everything, we are here to understand the laws of life by mastering the use of energy. Equipped with that skill and self-discipline, we will consciously advance on the road to eternity.

NATURAL IMPULSES AND Φ

From population growth and its estimate in large cities, to the human behavioural patterns reflected on the stock market, there is a constant appearance of numbers from the *Fibonacci series* as well as the tendency of numerous ratios to approximate to the *golden number* Φ. In the area of mathematical psychology **Vladimir Lefebvre**, the father of reflexive theory, has been searching for universal principles of brain function. He has shown that Φ appears in the ratio between the positive and negative evaluations of our opinions: 61.8% being our positive and 38.2% our average negative inclinations (61.8/38.2=1.618).

▶ *2.21 – How to teach BLISS to our heart and our brain? Science is already offering some solutions. – illustration by* **Daniel Winter**

EKG or EEG or...
Generalised in Principle Frequency Signature of Compression Path out of CHAOS!

Caduceus Compression
Perfect COMPRESSION-IMPLOSION
Golden Ratio Caduceus
Harmonic Cascade Identifies & Teaches BLISS/Transcendence & Self-Organisation in Brain Waves & Heart Waves
Heart Tuner: Bliss-Feedback as Science

Igniting DNA

IMPLOSION: Secret Science of Ecstasy & Immortality

Principles & Hygiene for BLISS Science

This ratio allows the mechanical energy of your squeezing love hug to 'cascade' right down until the tingle (spin) reaches your blood. 'Translating Vorticity' CAN be romantic!

Daniel Winter

Φ or Golden Mean ratio has been found in the frequency between harmonics of the heart at the moment of sending love, and (in the 'Sentics' measurement of emotion) in the ratio of the moment of maximum pressure in the shape of the hug or squeeze you give to send love...

The HUG THAT SAYS LOVE is one where the point of maximum pressure is approximately 0.618 or GOLDEN MEAN, into the duration of the hug or squeeze... What this says is that the love hug is explicitly more restrained initially, it is almost Tantric. Specifically, you don't go for the rush right away, you let it build.

Daniel Winter

In the early 1940s, the American engineer and accountant **Ralf Nelson Elliott** analysed the highs and lows of the stock market and found some regularities to be related to *Fibonacci numbers*. To him, it was obvious that nature's laws guide human activities and that human behavioural trends are reflected on the market. By observing price changes, **Elliott** noticed that two basic tendencies of human attitude, optimism and pessimism, express themselves in two major waves on the financial market. He called them *impulse waves* and *corrective waves* respectively. They are a mirror of social behaviour and **Elliott** concluded that they always create a specific and measurable pattern.

The *impulse wave*, which generally goes upwards, has five phases or smaller waves: three upwards and two downwards (Fig. 2.22). In the general downwards tendency of a *corrective wave* there are three phases, or smaller waves, two being downwards and one upwards. The numbers 1, 2, 3, 5 and 8 are from the *Fibonacci series*.

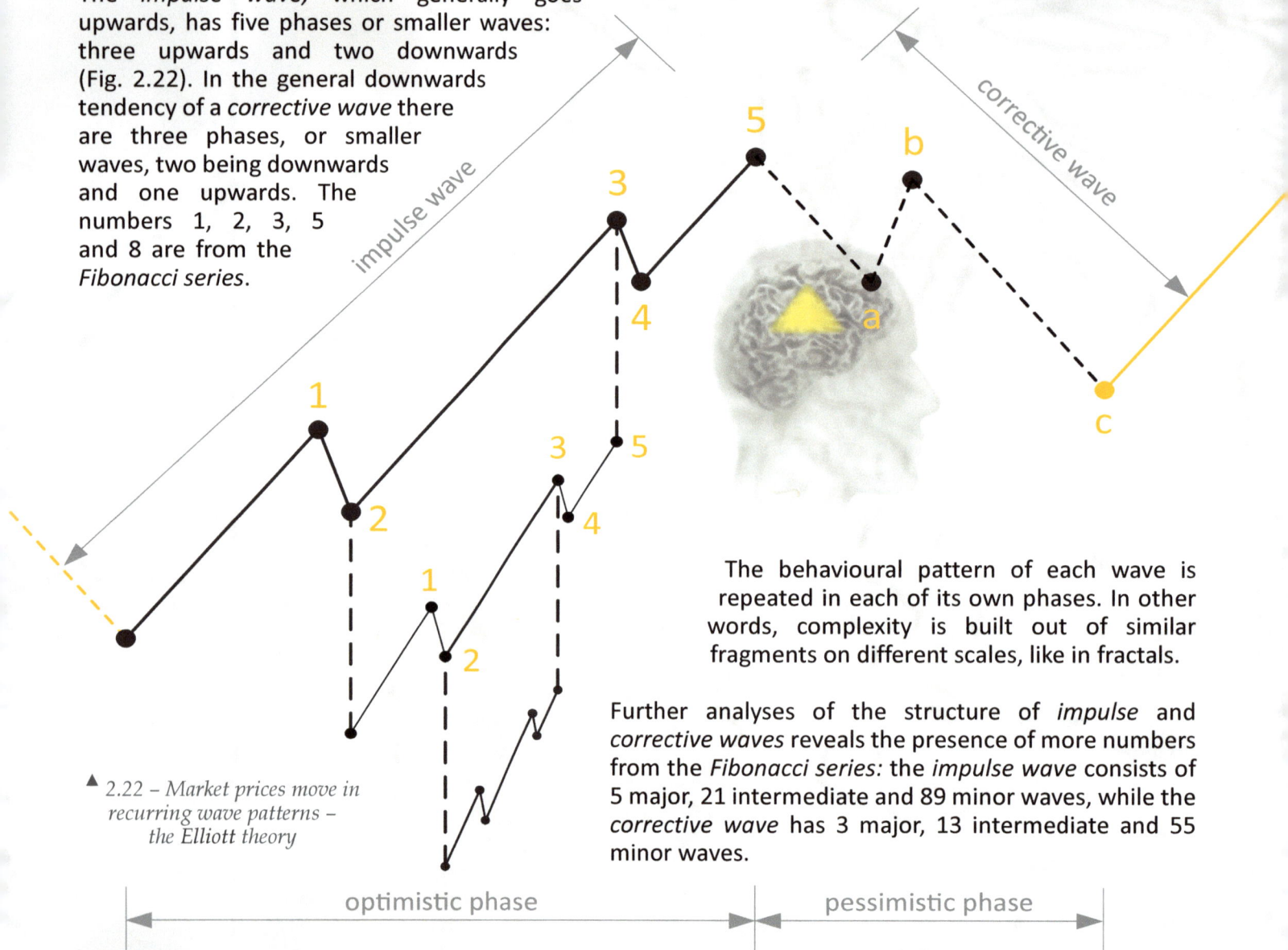

▲ *2.22 – Market prices move in recurring wave patterns – the Elliott theory*

The behavioural pattern of each wave is repeated in each of its own phases. In other words, complexity is built out of similar fragments on different scales, like in fractals.

Further analyses of the structure of *impulse* and *corrective waves* reveals the presence of more numbers from the *Fibonacci series*: the *impulse wave* consists of 5 major, 21 intermediate and 89 minor waves, while the *corrective wave* has 3 major, 13 intermediate and 55 minor waves.

optimistic phase — pessimistic phase

Recent research also indicated that in the flow of optimistic and pessimistic waves, Φ appears to be a determiner of the key turning points. It projects the pattern of human opinions and expectations onto another area of life, and that way we can observe how the environment may change while the ratio remains the same. This understanding of endless interconnectedness, constant mirroring, and of an inherent regulatory mechanism, may help us even to run businesses more successfully.

The wisdom of ages past never loses its relevance: *post nubila phoebus (after clouds, the sun)*. A period of prosperity inevitably heads towards a point of decline, and decline after some time breeds motivation to succeed. When the cycle is played through and completed, another one starts. This is nature's rhythm as well as the rhythm of human behaviour. Acknowledging it in his theory, **Elliott** revealed how the relationship between social phenomena and their inner phases can be described through the *Fibonacci numbers* and Φ.

LOOK AT THE MARIGOLD

> All human activities have three distinctive features: pattern, time and ratio, all of which observe the Fibonacci summation series.
>
> Ralf Nelson Elliott

> It is important that you understand that you create the future and you cannot risk speaking angers, speaking judgements, speaking darkness against another, yourself, your family, your government, your world, or your God. For it will be instrumental in the next shift to come.
>
> through
> Gillian MacBeth-Louthan[II-9]
> (Quantum Newsletter)

> Nobody should say that His own invisibility God uses on our expense and that He has stayed completely unknown to people. On the contrary, He has brought His Creation to the order from which about Him, despite His natural invisibility, an awareness based on His deeds can be obtained.
>
> Athanasius of Alexandria

In the plant world we also find the *Fibonacci series* and the *golden number* Φ. There are plants where the number of branches in each successive generation follows a progression through the *Fibonacci series* (Fig. 2.23, 2.25). Since Φ is present in the regular pentagon/pentagram, the plants that have flowers made of five petals often have *golden number* Φ inherent in their geometry. The flowers of edible fruits, for example, have five petals so it seems that Five indicates acceptable food. Five is present in the structure of organic forms, while geometry based on *six* and *eight* dominates the world of minerals and inanimate forms.

Plants with a geometry based on *six* are either poisonous or are cautiously used by herbalists, while those based on the geometry of *seven* are considered poisonous. Despite this fact, the so-called *nightshade* vegetables: *the Solanaceae family (white potatoes, tomatoes, aubergines)* and *the Capsicum family (green* and *red peppers* and *chilli peppers)*, are all largely consumable. They contain toxins which destroy red blood cells and have been connected with a long list of problems like kidney stones, ulcers, rheumatoid arthritis, breathing problems, digestive problems, skin problems, nerve and energy problems.

If we cut a fruit or vegetable, the number of sections they have is often a number of the *Fibonacci series*. For example, a *banana, melon* and *cucumber,* have three sections whereas an *apple* has five. Also, the number of petals in a flower is often a number from the *Fibonacci series* or one very close to it, like: *Lilies, Iris* – 3, *Buttercups, Wild Rose* – 5, *Delphinium* – 8, *Corn Marigold* – 13, *Black-eyed Susan, Chicory* – 21.

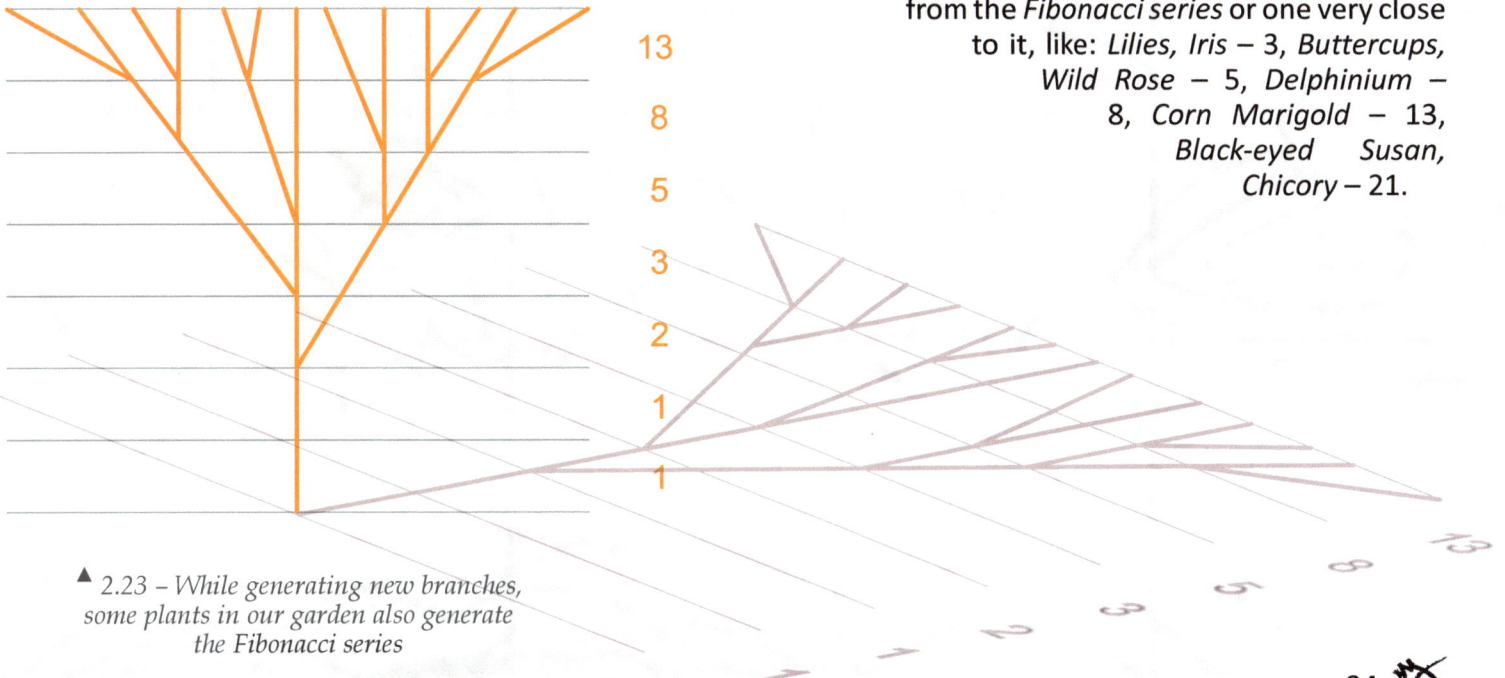

▲ 2.23 – *While generating new branches, some plants in our garden also generate the Fibonacci series*

Numbers from the *Fibonacci series* also appear in the structure of the body of many animals. In the morphology of insects, we see the body divided into three major sections: the head, thorax and abdomen. The thorax has three parts, with wings and three pairs of legs attached to it, while the abdomen is composed of eight segments. Extremities are divided into three and eight parts, and the head in some, like in mosquitoes, is equipped with five antennae. All these numbers are from the *Fibonacci series* and they appear even in the pattern and colour alterations in the wings of some butterflies.

Certain *turtles,* for example, have thirteen horny plates in the central part of their shell; five being surrounded by eight. They also have 34 vertebrae. *Fibonacci numbers* are present in the skeletal structure of mammals as well. For example, the number of skeleton bones tends to be 34 *(deer)* or 55 *(whale)*. Domestic animals have nearly, or exactly, 55 vertebrae and 13 pairs of ribs while *cats, dogs* and *pigs* have 89 chest bones. The sum of the bones and teeth in many is close to 233.

All of life seems to be mathematically explainable or, shall we say, coded. The most apparently random phenomena exhibit striking orderliness if studied within a wide enough scope. Nothing is exempt, not even the total number of young rabbits in each new generation. In ideal circumstances, it is a number in the *Fibonacci series*. We can see how even natural impulses, established by the Creator, are ordered through the *golden number Φ*.

Everywhere around us, as well as inside us, the *golden proportion* is on constant duty as a keeper of order, harmony and beauty. A walk through a meadow, or an animal park, is like a walk through a museum of nature's perfection. Now we can approach that perfection with a new understanding of how we fit into it. One glance at the flower is enough to convey to us a direct love message from God and connect us with the Whole. The truth is always ever so simple.

The abundance of the *golden proportion* in nature and its presence in our body reveal a common creational principle applied on all levels. It is the principle of harmonious connection of parts with their whole.

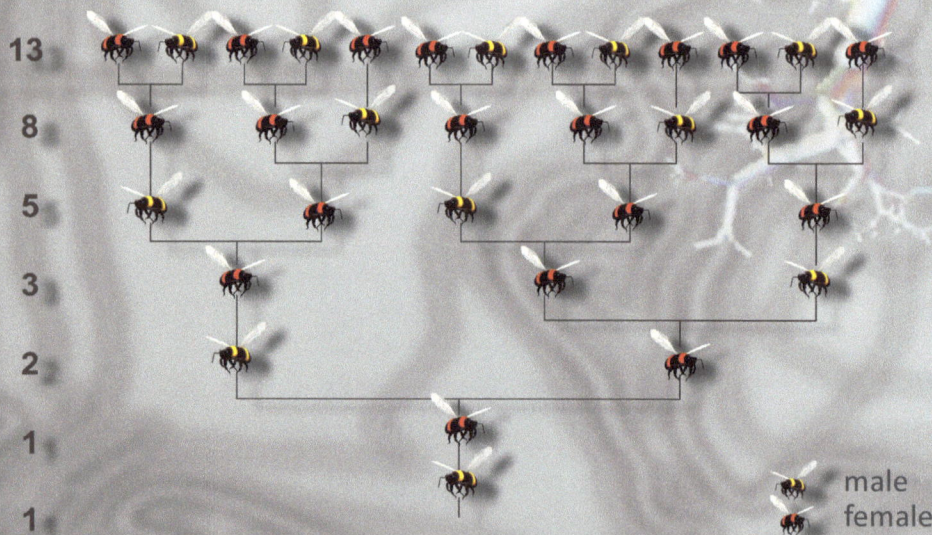

male
female

▲ 2.24 – *The family tree of any bee branches in the accumulative growth pattern of the Fibonacci series: 1, 1, 2, 3, 5, 8, 13, 21..., which also illustrates the breeding pattern of rabbits and the branching of some trees (Fig. 2.23, 2.25).*

GOLDEN PROPORTION MANIFESTED

ART AND IMMORTALITY

ARCHITECTURE AND PAINTINGS

Proportionality of form, regardless of whether it is aural or visual, makes a big impact on the emotional perception of its composition. Researches have shown if the parts of a form relate through the *golden number Φ,* the form is highly pleasing. This applies to all arts.

The *golden proportion* is a mathematical concept the study of which belongs primarily to science. However, at the same time it is a measure of harmony and therefore as a criterion of beauty it also belongs to art and aesthetics. Thus Φ connects science and art.

In ancient civilisations such as Egypt, Greece and China then through the Renaissance and later periods, the *golden proportion* was appreciated and used in various art forms. The position of the key compositional elements in **Leonardo da Vinci**'s painting *The Last Supper* was determined by the use of the *golden proportion,* while the French impressionist painter **Georges Seurat** was said to have approached every canvas with the *golden proportion* first. **Salvador Dali**, who was a student of ancient art, often dealt with Φ when incorporating pentagonal symmetry in his work.

The Great Pyramid in Egypt, the front façade of the Parthenon in Athens and the west façade of the Notre Dame in Paris, are all famous for the presence of the *golden proportion*. Another example is the French Cathedral in Chartres, a unique treasure of *sacred geometry* that has been astonishing and inspiring generations of builders. Amongst modern architectural works, the main block of the United Nations building in New York is composed of three *golden rectangles*.

2.25 – The morphology of natural organisms is designed with mathematical precision – illustration by Sándor Kabai

Without mathematics – there is no art.

Luca Pacioli

Art is the manifestation of sacred laws of nature, which, without art, could never come to expression.

Goethe[II-10]

The main elements of beauty are order, symmetry, definite limitation, and they are the chief properties that the mathematical science draws attention to.

Aristotle[II-11]

We are so left-brain oriented – logical, rational, and intellectual, that we think all understanding must arise from this mode of consciousness; even to the extent of viewing art and looking for what it represents. The hidden mysteries of the universe can never be understood by this mode of comprehension alone.

Dr Noel Huntley[II-12]

The fact that in paintings we often find the line of the horizon of a landscape picture, or eyes of a person in a portrait, positioned at the point of the *golden proportion,* or other cardinal elements of composition related through Φ, does not mean it is always the artists' conscious choice. Rather, artists intuitively recognise nature's principles of harmony and record them in their work. That ability illustrates artists' proximity both to nature and their inner selves.

Since the *golden proportion* reigns throughout the natural world, and we as beings are a phenomenon of nature, the structural harmony of natural systems is our own harmony too. Natural beauty has the potential to excite our senses while rejuvenating our biology, and that is beyond dispute. Thus by recognising harmony in nature, through the law of resonance we stimulate our inner harmony. The higher the resonance between these two systems, outer and inner, the more explicit and purer is the beauty of the resulting artwork.

About a hundred years ago, in his book *The Curves of Life,* **Theodore Andrea Cook** stated: *I venture, in fact, to offer Φ as an underlying reason for what we call Beauty both in a natural object and in a masterpiece of art*. This observation seems to indicate the recognition of a common numerical constant for nature and arts.

The golden ratio of 1.618 expressed as the ultimate proportion of harmony, beauty and spirituality was used in the design of sacred buildings in Ancient Architecture to produce spiritual energy that facilitated connectivity with spiritual realms through resonant prayer. Popular among spiritually significant shapes are pyramids and hemispheres (e.g. the domes, that are the basis of religious buildings, be it a mosque, a church or a synagogue). These particular shapes are energy emitters; they are shapes that produce a type of penetrating carrier wave which Chaumery and De Belizal named negative green.

Dr Ibrahim F. Karim[(II-13)]

SILENT RECONNECTING

Throughout history in the area of architecture, particularly sacred buildings, designers practised their understanding of the divine harmony by applying the principles of *sacred geometry*. Consequently, the life-force structured through *sacred geometry* gives to these buildings a unique quality, beauty and power. That is the very reason people are attracted to the sacred sites.

▲ *2.26 – A harmonic decomposition of a square through Φ is often used as a matrix for design*

If you operate and build through Sacred Geometry, exactly through the rules of Sacred Geometry, then you will create something that creates a positive flow. There are many things on this planet that create a positive flow, and many things that create a negative flow, but in this new golden Age the recognition of a positive energy flow in the buildings that are designed and built or machinery that is built, will create more harmony. Negative flow will be disallowed by Spirit within the next few years; you will be able to see that buildings that create a negative flow of energy will become unsafe and will fall down completely.

Kryon
through David Brown

The more easily we perceive the order which characterises the objects contemplated, the more simple and more perfect will they appear, and the more easily and joyfully shall we acknowledge them. But an order which costs trouble to discover, although it will indeed also please us, will associate with that pleasure a certain degree of weariness and sadness.

Helmholtz(II-14)

▶ *2.27 – God and Me – the meeting scheduled aeons ago*

The harmonised energy of sacred buildings is compatible with, pleasurable and nourishing to the human energy field, because a man is part of the same life-force and was designed according to the same rules of geometry. Our experience of a sacred reconnection is thus triggered when we visit those buildings and sites. We smoothly slide into a divine energy field familiar to our latent godliness, and it is no wonder that at sacred sites we feel like we were back Home. These sites facilitate our process of embedding into the divine fractal of sacred energies highly charged with the life-force.

Nowadays scientific explanations enrich this arena by bringing new light to the connection between the mundane and the sacred. The Egyptian architect **Dr Ibrahim F. Karim**, after years of research, revealed that certain shapes, or geometries, emit vibrations that charge space with life-force. The ancients in some ways possessed that knowledge which they implemented in the design of their sacred buildings. As a result, these spaces reinforce the human energy field with purifying energies, facilitating our connection with the Divine.

Symmetry is one of the principles extensively applied in sacred buildings, and modern physics is aware of the fact that symmetry contributes towards sustainability throughout life. Sustainability means endurance through reconciliation. It is a formula for continuous constructive unity and a formula for eternity.

Sacred buildings, and all art work, are forms of human creation which are infused with the purest energies. By experiencing them we come closer to the Creator, to His perfection, to our self-truth.

The scientific aspect of Sacred Geometry is saying: yes, there exists an underlying system or method, an inner harmony of Creation where all is in a state of infinite connectedness. This is the meaning of 'uni-verse', 'uni-son(g)'... It is the dimensionless or transcendent side of reality, and hence the science there is one of ratio alone (which is dimension-less, or pure symmetry) and not one of quantities like 'meter' or 'kilogram' (which are dimensional attributes). This subtle science of the inner harmony of creation is mathematically based upon the famous 'Golden Mean ratio', and here it is not a question of beauty alone. Clearly our world is one of dimensions and unison.

Frank van den Bovenkamp (Heart Coherence team)

Why does the *golden proportion*, epitomized in artwork and inherent in nature, make such a big impression on us?

Φ is a common denominator of the physical (manifested) and the incomprehensible (*irrational number*), since it dwells in both realms. As infinite beings operating in a confined physical world, we exist in these two realms, too. Ancient philosophers saw the human being as a microcosm made in an image of the macrocosm. Mirroring is believed to be done on both the physical and subtle inner levels of our being. Having the Φ embedded in our entire morphology as our divine inheritance, we are enabled by virtue of our design to resonate with the Φ acting around us.

The moment we recognise beauty is the moment when our inherent godliness starts resonating with its source. Consciousness that loves all Creation equally, because of the Creator, finds beauty and joy in everything.

Φ AND MUSIC

In search of deeper coherence and stronger harmonies in their work, some composers intuitively come up with the *golden proportion* while some others use it deliberately. Many classical composers like **Chopin** (each of the 24 preludes, op. 28), **Schubert**, **Mozart** and **J. S. Bach** in some of their works, used the *golden proportion* knowingly as part of their design and therefore a tool towards greater integrity in their compositions.

Debussy used the *Fibonacci numbers* 8, 13, 21, and 34 to organise sections in the music of *Image, Reflections in Water*. The form and proportion of **Bela Bartok**'s *Six string quartets* are structured according to the *Fibonacci series* and the *golden proportion* to create an overall pattern of aesthetically pleasing music. For example, in his *Music for Strings, Percussion and Celeste* intervals marked by *Fibonacci numbers* (1:2:3:5:8:5:3:2:1) guide xylophone progression. In **Beethoven**'s *Fifth Symphony* the famous opening motif is repeated at the point of the *golden proportion* (0.618) of the whole symphony.

In the case of modern music, like *pop* and *rock*, some analyses of the harmonic structure of the song *Child in Time*, by **Deep Purple**, show evidence of the *golden proportion* but it is still argued whether it was used knowingly or intuitively.

Some elements of the piano keyboard are also connected to the *Fibonacci series*. These are the white and the black keys that make an *octave*. The eight white keys mark natural notes while the five black keys, grouped in twos and threes, mark their so-called *sharp* or *flat* variations. The numbers 2, 3, 5, 8, and 13, are *Fibonacci numbers*.

Emotion is magnetism. Sound enlivens emotion. Emotion attracts new realities into form. The emotional magnetism of Divine Music powerfully attracts Heaven and Love into manifestation on Earth.

Music is the language of emotion. Music soothes and uplifts the soul, it is the universal language that transcends all barriers, in all dimensions and planes.

Music is the language of the heavenly hosts, and of the Angels, who are messengers of Divine Love and Will for the highest good of ALL.

Angels of Music – Soteri[(II-7)]

The constant ratio 1.618 of the 'golden' division, expressed with rather small error as ratios of the integer numbers 8:5, 5:3, 3:2, corresponds to numerical values of consonance intervals of the octave, the diminished sixth, the sixth, and the quint.

Prof. Grimm
(Proportionality in the Architecture)

▲ *2.28 – All paths are One Path, stretched between the past and future eternities*

In poetry there are records, as early as Roman times, documenting the use of the *golden proportion*. **Dante Alighiery** (1265-1321) applied it in his famous *Divine Comedy*.

Later on, in the early 19th century, one of the greatest Russian poets **A. S. Pushkin** (1799-1837) structured some of his work using the numbers from the *Fibonacci series*. According to the research by the famous Russian film director and theorist **S. M. Eisenstein** (1898-1948), in *Ruslan and Ludmila* **Pushkin** usually made plot twists at the points of the *golden proportion*. **Eisenstein** would, for example, find them in line 13 within a 21-line verse.

The body is the garment of the soul and it is the soul which gives life to the voice. That's why the body must raise its voice in harmony with the soul for the praise of God...For all the arts serving human desires and needs are derived from the breath that God sent into the human body.

Hildegard of Bingen[II-15]
(Book of Divine Works)

If a wave or a heartbeat or a person as nests of waves, were to re-occur re-cursively forever, than that would be SUSTAINABILITY or 'eternal recursion' or literally IMMORTALITY – wouldn't it?

Daniel Winter

Evolvement is a Phenomenon gained by a Human Being's attaining Satiety for everything.

*Vedia Bülent
(Önsü) Çorak
(Light)*

Another example is the last prince-bishop of Montenegro, **Petar II Petrović Njegoš** (1813-1851), a foremost South Slavic poet. He appreciated numbers and extensively applied the *Fibonacci series,* and the *golden proportion,* in his work. **Njegoš** understood proportion and symmetry, and with a profound use of numbers he created a harmonious relationship between the form and content in his writing. Hence, for example, in his masterpiece *The Light of Microcosm,* when structuring rhymes, he chose adjacent numbers from the *Fibonacci series* for the number of lines in a stanza so that the stanzas would relate through the *golden number*. Complying with the universal principles of order, he believed the internal harmony of his lines would echo the ever-lasting perfection of *All That Is*.

CHANGE IS EVOLVEMENT

The harmonic unity of the Creation, exemplified by the *golden proportion* inside and outside us, pervades us with its power. Through the accord of their proportions, particularly through the *golden proportion,* sacred buildings provide a charge as a form of vitality they unceasingly offer to their visitors. Despite changes in the energy of time, this lasting property makes them attractive for hundreds and even thousands of years. In view of the fact that charge-attraction supports life, and by looking at the ways and places we spend our life in, also at the food we eat and habits we have, we could determine whether we are on the road to immortality or to self-destruction. Responsibility for our own selves is in our own hands.

Life is mainly determined by the chain of decisions we make. The matter of our choice is whether we are going to consciously speed up our evolution or slow it down by resorting to the old patterns we feel comfortable with. Since from the higher point of view there is nothing but change, and every change is a particular evolvement, we cannot escape growth however slow or unconscious it may be.

From the open sky, more intensively than ever, energies of the unknown universal depths and layers of the universal knowledge are showering us stimulating our evolvement codes. So, the road to travel is lit with the growing body of light/information for the pleasure of those open to change and aware of the need to evolve. It does not mean that life is becoming easier but that the whole journey can become more conscious and our evolvement faster.

GOLDEN PROPORTION

I-1   Plato (Πλάτων, 427BC-347BC), is considered one of the most significant ancient Greek philosophers. Plato's Academy was built in 428BC, in Athens, on a site continuously inhabited since prehistoric times. The philosophical school gained fame thanks to the Neoplatonists. It existed for more than seven centuries, before Emperor Justinian closed it in the year 347AD.

I-2   Daniel Winter, a writer and lecturer in the areas of electrical engineering, psychophysiology (the origin of languages), computer animation in multimedia and non-linear energy source technologies. Winter developed superior technology for measuring coherent emotions in the heart *(HeartTuner, also called BlissTuner)*. In his research and practical work he bridges the physical with the metaphysical; www.fractalfield.com

I-3   Jain, born in Australia to Lebanese parents, is the author of 12 books and 6 DVDs on ancient knowledge in the areas of *Vedic mathematics*, *magic squares*, *sacred geometry*, *divine proportion* and the *Platonic solids*. As a theatrical director he developed a maths enrichment programme for schools called *MatheMagics*. Through a performance called *The Theatre of the Holy Numbers*, mathematics is taught through a play in which actors wear elaborate costumes. Jain has been lecturing in schools and universities around Australia for more than 15 years. He authored many exhibitions on mathematical art, and is also a healer/herbalist and muralist; www.jainmathemagics.com

I-4   An in-depth investigation of π, Φ and the number 33, by Joseph Edward Batter and Stephen Langton Goulet, can be found on their website 'The Lix Unit': www.lixcaliber.com

I-5   See chapter *GOLDEN PROPORTION MANIFESTED, Φ and the geometry of the human body,* page 29

I-6   *The Knowledge Book,* given through Vedia Bülent (Önsü) Çorak, contains the frequencies of all sacred books, revealed to our planet so far, together with the frequency of the *Mighty Energy Focal Point*. It is a *Universal Constitution* of the *Lordly order* also called the *Golden Book of the Golden Age* or the *Book of Truth*. All references relate to hardcover book (Second Edition, January 1998); www.dkb-mevlana.org.tr

GOLDEN PROPORTION MANIFESTED

II-1 Rick D. Howard, in 2003, developed a mathematical theory that showed the presence of the *irrational numbers Φ, π* and *e* – the base to the natural logarithm, in the design of the *Great Pyramid* in Egypt. This theory also reveals that the same constants are present in some other ancient monuments.

II-2 Messages from The GROUP first came to Steve Rother in 1996. Translated into 11 languages so far, they have filled several books since (see the back cover). The monthly *Beacons of Light – Reminders from Home* have been translated into 21 languages and presented at the United Nations five times; www.lightworker.com

II-3 Frank van den Bovenkamp, *Heart Coherence team;* www.heartcoherence.com

II-4 Sheldan Nidle is a representative and lecturer for the *Galactic Federation of Light*. He founded the *Planetary Activation Organization (PAO)* in November 1997; www.paoweb.com

II-5 Kryon – from the message channelled on 1st January 2003 through David Brown; kryon.org.za

II-6 Sándor Kabai is a mechanical engineer specialising in aviation and manufacturing technology. He is a member of the Geometry and Space Research Team – an inter-disciplinary group hosted by the Academy of Sciences and various universities in Hungary. On his website complex mathematical graphics can be found; www.kabai.hu

II-7 Messages from Angels; www.star-knowledge.net

II-8 V. I. Korobko and G. I. Korobko, *The golden proportion and a Man*; Caucasian Library Publishing House, Stavropol, 1995

II-9 Gillian MacBeth-Louthan is a clairvoyant psychic, a metaphysical teacher, messenger and internationally known medium. For over 35 years she has been working with the *Councils of Light, Mary Magdalene, Merlin, White Buffalo Calf Woman, Mother Mary, Pleiadians* and many other energies of the Christ Light; www.thequantumawakening.com

II-10 Johann Wolfgang Von Göethe (1749-1832), was a German cultural icon and a polymath with interests and accomplishments in the visual arts, music, drama, poetry, politics, science and philosophy. He was also a polyglot fluent in French, Italian, English, Latin, Greek and Hebrew, and he translated works of Byron and Voltaire. Göethe became famous at the age of 25 when he wrote *The Sorrows of Young Werther*. In 1794 he met Friedrich Schiller and their lasting friendship made a permanent mark on German culture. Göethe's most enduring work, and one of the greatest creations in world literature, was the poetic drama *Faustus* (1808). He is as celebrated in Germany as Shakespeare is in England.

II-11 Aristotle (Αριστοτέλης, 384BC-322BC), together with Socrates (470BC-399BC) and Plato (Πλάτων, 427BC-347BC), is considered one of the most significant ancient Greek philosophers. Aristotle was Plato's student and a teacher of Alexander the Great. His interests embraced all available knowledge and Aristotle was the encyclopaedia-man of his time. He studied and wrote on topics of science, philosophy, education, literature and poetry. Some of his most important works are *Physics, Metaphysics* (or *Ontology), Nicomachean Ethics, Politics, De Anima (On the Soul)* and *Poetics*. Aristotle favoured the empirical way of evaluating data rather than the *a priori* way of intuition or revelation, and thus laid a foundation for the methodology of modern science.

II-12   Noel Huntley, PhD, English scientist with a background in physics and doctorates in psychology and parapsychology, also a talented painter and musician, with a keen interest in computers. He has developed the foundation for a spiritual science as well as for the physics of a higher dimensional consciousness. Some of his books are: *ET and ALIENS: Who Are They? And Why Are They Here?*; *The Scientific Principles of Spiritual Enslavement* and *Attainment of Superior Physical Abilities and the New Science of Body Motion.* His website *Beyond Duality* is a collection of articles on variety of topics, like evolution, the nature of time, ascension, consciousness, holographic civilisation, fractals, types of physics and the theory of one; www.users.globalnet.co.uk/~noelh

II-13   Ibrahim F. Karim, PhD, Egyptian architect, the father of the new science of BioGeometry™. With Rawya Karim, MA, he founded the *BioGeometrical Systems Institute Company* in 1993 as a design centre for research and implementation of BioGeometry™; www.biogeometry.com

II-14   Herman Ludwig Ferdinand Von Helmholtz (1821-1894) was a German physician and physicist entirely devoted to science. While studying muscle metabolism, he discovered the energy conservation principle. He contributed to the field of sensory physiology as well as medical optics by inventing an instrument to examine the inside of the human eye. With his book *On the sensations of tone as a physiological basis for the theory of music* he enriched the studies of sound and aesthetics. After 1871, the year Helmholtz moved to Berlin to become a professor of physics, his interest in electromagnetism resulted in the *theory of waves* and the first ever demonstration of electromagnetic radiation.

II-15   Hildegard of Bingen (1098-1179), was a powerful female figure in the German medieval church who earned the title of saint. She was a mystic, author, composer, teacher and monastic leader. At the age of eight Hildegard was sent to a monastery. Having had visions from early years, she recognised her innermost need to preserve those experiences in writing. Consequently, she compiled her visions in three books: *Scivias (Know the Way)*, *Liber Vitae meritorum (Book of Life's Merits)* and *De operatione Dei (Of God's Activities,* also known as the *Book of Divine Works).* About eighty compositions from her musical opus have survived and one of the better known is *Ordo Virtutum (Order of Virtues).*

II-16   All attempts by the author to reveal the originator, and to contact the originator/guardian of this figure, have been to no avail. The same applies to the illustrations featured in figure 2.19. If you have information about them, please contact the author via the publishers in order to give proper acknowledgement.

Front cover: Detail of the *Dimension of the All-Truthful*
Graphic design of the book: zodrag@gmail.com

BIBLIOGRAPHY

ANTI-GRAVITY & THE WORLD GRID, edited by David Hatcher Childress; Adventures Unlimited Press

- THE ANCIENT SECRETS OF THE FLOWER OF LIFE, Volume 1 & 2 by Drunvalo Melchizedek; Sedona Color Graphics
- A BEGINNER'S GUIDE TO CONSTRUCTING THE UNIVERSE – The mathematical archetypes of Nature, Art, and Science a voyage from 1 to 10 by Michael S. Schneider; Harper Perennial, a division of Harper Collins Publishers
- CELTIC SPIRALS – handbook by Sheila Sturrock; Guild of Master Craftsman Publication Ltd
- FENG SHUI – The Traditional Oriental Way to Enhance Your Life by Stephen Skinner; Siena book, an imprint of Parragon
- THE FRACTAL GEOMETRY OF NATURE by Benoit B. Mandelbrot; W. H. Freeman and Company, New York
- THE GEOMETRY OF ART AND LIFE by Matila Ghyka; Dover Publications, inc. New York
- HIDDEN NATURE – The Startling Insights of Viktor Schauberger by Alick Bartholomew; Floris Books
- THE IMPLOSIONS' GRAND ATTRACTOR – Sacred Geometry & Coherent Emotion; assembled, Edited & Distributed from Daniel Winter's writing by Implosion Group
- ISLAMIC PATTERNS – An Analytical and Cosmological Approach by Keith Critchlow; Thames and Hudson, London
- JUST SIX NUMBERS – The Deep Forces that Shape the Universe by Martin Rees; Weidenfeld & Nicolson – London
- THE KNOWLEDGE BOOK – Messages received and transformed into writing by Vedia Bülent (Önsü) Çorak; World Brotherhood Union Mevlana Supreme Foundation, Istanbul
- L' ASTROLOGIE SACRE – Miroir de la Grande Tradition, Frederic Lionel; Editions du Rocher, Monaco
- LET THE NUMBERS GUIDE YOU – The Spiritual Science of Numerology by Shiv Charan Singh; O Books, Winchester, UK; New York, USA
- MAGIC SYMBOLS by Frederick Goodman; Brian Trodd Publishing House Limited
- THE MASTER MASONS OF CHARTRES by John James; West Grinstead Publishing
- NATURE'S NUMBERS – Discovering Order And Pattern In The Universe by Ian Stewart; Weidenfeld & Nicolson – London
- NUMEROLOGY with Tantra, Ayurveda, and Astrology – A Key to Human Behaviour by Harish Johari; Destiny Books, Rochester, Vermont
- ORDER IN SPACE – A Design Source Book by Keith Critchlow; Thames and Hudson, London
- PATTERN AND DESIGN WITH DYNAMIC SYMMETRY – How to Create Art Deco Geometrical Design by Edward B. Edwards; Dover Publications, inc, New York
- RANDOMNESS by Deborah J. Bennett; Harvard University Press, Cambridge, Massachusetts, London England
- SACRED GEOMETRY by Miranda Lundy; Wooden Books Ltd
- SACRED GEOMETRY – Philosophy and practice by Robert Lawlor; Thames and Hudson
- SECRETS OF ANCIENT AND SACRED PLACES – The world's Mysterious Heritage by Paul Devereux; Brockhampton Press, London
- SUNLIGHT ON WATER – A Manual for Soul-full Living – The One With No Names through Flo Aeveia Magdalena
- SYMMETRY IN CHAOS – A Search for Pattern in mathematics, Art and Nature by Michael Field and Martin Golubitsky; Oxford University Press
- THE JOY OF PI by David Plather; Bath Press Colourbooks, Glasgow
- THE SECRET SCIENCE OF ECSTASY AND IMMORTALITY – IMPLOSION by Daniel Winter
- THE TRUE POWER OF WATER – Healing And Discovering Ourselves by Masaru Emoto; Beyond Words Publishing, Inc., Hillsboro, Oregon
- YANTRA – The Tantric Symbol of Cosmic Unity by Madhu Khanna; Thames and Hudson

Published by
M PUBLISHING
www.memento13.com

A catalogue record for this book is available from
the British Library

ISBN
978-1-909323-06-3